Carole Lazarus and Jennifer Berman

# GLORAFILIA
## THE IMPRESSIONISTS IN NEEDLEPOINT

'In the France of the Impressionists, serious art was regarded as a male stronghold. Girls were groomed in 'feminine' accomplishments: music, a little gentle watercoloring, needlework. Needlework, actually, was considered a prescription of good sense, attitude and behavior. So . . . straight backs, neatly crossed ankles. Let's begin!'

CAROLE LAZARUS AND JENNIFER BERMAN

# GLORAFILIA

## THE IMPRESSIONISTS IN NEEDLEPOINT

CROWN PUBLISHERS, INC.
New York

For Harvey and Geoff – who have made such an impression!

Special photography by Tim Imrie

Edited by Emma Callery and Gillian Haslam
Designed by Polly Dawes
Styling by Cathy Sinker
Illustrations by King and King

Title page picture: *Lydia working at a tapestry frame*, Mary Cassatt, c. 1881.

Typeset in Times by Textype Typesetters, Cambridge
Color separations using environmentally friendly inks by Magnacraft,
London
Printed and bound in Italy by New Interlitho S.p.a., Milan

Papers used by Ebury Press are natural, recyclable products made from
wood grown in sustainable forests.

Published by Crown Publishers, Inc., 201 East 50th Street, New York,
New York 10022. Member of the Crown Publishing Group.

Random House, Inc. New York, Toronto, London, Sydney, Auckland

Originally published in Great Britain by Ebury Press in 1993.

CROWN is the trademark of Crown Publishers, Inc.

Manufactured in Italy

Library of Congress Cataloging-in-Publication Data is available upon
request.

ISBN: 0-517-59223-1

10 9 8 7 6 5 4 3 2 1

First American Edition

# CONTENTS

# INTRODUCTION

'Five or six lunatics, including a woman, a group of unhappy souls mad with ambition, exhibited at the Galerie Durand-Ruel. There are people who burst out laughing on seeing such things. As for me, it wrings my heart. These so-called artists call themselves Intransigents, Impressionists, they take canvas, color and brushes, haphazardly throw a few tones on the surface and sign the whole . . . a frightful spectacle of human vanity lost to the point of madness.'

Albert Wolff, *Le Figaro*, 3 April 1876

Once upon a time there lived in France, in various stages of anonymity, recognition, poverty, elation and despair, the group of painters described above. What would the collective noun be – an Inspiration of Impressionists, a Perception of Impressionists? It has been suggested, tongue slightly in cheek, that although they were credited as visionaries, maybe they were just a bunch of artists with defective eyesight. Whatever your opinion, they painted many of the world's most beautiful images, and most of them lived to hear the ridicule silenced. We have put some of these images into needlepoint, and in doing so, interest became respect, respect became fascination, and this in turn became a true labor of love.

This book happened in a time warp, the year both elastic and evaporating. Our previous book *Glorafilia: The Venice Collection*, was plucked from the ether of whimsy, whereas this one began in a footsore, rain-soaked way at the hotel in Paris where Oscar Wilde 'died beyond his means', progressed via scorching bouts of photography in France, and ended with the office's return to normality. The group who had shared the year, coming and going, Pissarro over by the word processor, Manet propped on his cane examining his cuticles, were told 'Thanks, guys'. The squirrel's nest of glorious new yarns collated itself obediently onto shelves, the reference books were closed, 31 December had the deadline word '*Fin*' scrawled across it, and there were no partridges in pear trees for us that Christmas. It was a year of global rejoicings and disasters, of personal tragedies and pleasures, of children beginning to travel ('Will you accept a collect call from Agra, from Bangkok?'). We get older but, working in such a close partnership, don't see it in each other, only the galloping of the seasons, of events.

During the year the Old Mill House, our shop and company base, threatened to crumble and needed major silicone implants, liposuction and spinal surgery. For months we lived encased in scaffolding to stop our beautiful listed building listing irredeemably down the Mill Field and into the sunset. The original brickwork and windows were painstakingly recreated, the preservation society peered over the girders, and we learned

*Monet's garden at Giverny explodes in a spectacular celebration of Spring. He painted the irises in 1900 (the needlepoint picture this inspired was done some time later).*

the intimate details of the lives of the decorators, delivered *con brio* up the stair . . .'She didn't!' 'She bloody did!'. Their paint-rollers swept regardless across handles and light switches, and in a parallel universe Renoir experimented with impasto paint effects; the decorators poked paint into tiny holes and Pissarro strayed into pointillisme.

The Impressionists created such mouth-watering paintings that initially we thought it would be easy to choose what we wanted. The opposite was true. The conjuring trick that works so spontaneously in paint would have insulted the artist in needlepoint. Some pictures were sewn, unpicked, resewn, unpicked . . . the delicate shading in the nape of a neck, achieved in seconds with a flicking brush stroke, could take hours of experimenting on canvas. We tried to convey a feeling, we simplified, edited, exaggerated, we used glorious yarns that would mix and shade – wools, cottons, metallic threads and more than a handful of artistic licence.

We endured great hardships for this book. We travelled in freak heatwaves and freak storms. We visited modest farmhouses where the Impressionists stayed to find them multi-starred hotels, compelling us for old times' sake to eat through several courses. We shared a beautiful château bedroom with a battlefield of photographic paraphernalia, we shared a room in Honfleur with an undisposable piece of fermenting cheese, and have sampled toilets great and small. The days we spent in Monet's gardens at Giverny should be spread over a lifetime – like very rich chocolates to be taken as necessary, not all at once. Those days stay in the memory as permanently as the daffodils did on Wordsworth's inner eye.

We think of the Impressionists in a way that suggests a harmonious group. Some were friends, some were not. At different times they influenced each other, interacted, inspired, but they were quite disparate. They had one thing in common, which gains them entry into the hallowed ranks: they were the last ties with traditional and identifiable painting before the moorings were severed. In short, they saw things differently and in doing so the familiar became unfamiliar and the world of paintings was turned on its head.

We picture most of the group in maturity, bearded, looking worn, somber, weighted with years. Perhaps we should try to see them young, on fire, radical, the nineteenth century equivalent of today's frayed, earringed, booted, shaven-headed, dreadlocked or beribboned creators, with the same excitements and energies, and similarly in need of a soup kitchen.

The Impressionists were mainly middle class, from families of distinction or successful merchants, one or two from aristocracy, some made poor by reduced circumstances or the severing of family links. Only Renoir had a modest upbringing, while Pissarro was the only one blessed with a Jewish mother. Imagine the conversation: 'A painter? Do you want to give your father a heart attack?'

The prevailing attitude to art was that it had already been defined, as far back as the Greeks, and that was that. They all grew up with the official Salon esteemed as a quality yardstick, were generally refused entry, and did all they could to win official recognition because this was the only way of making a living. Many of them sacrificed all material quality of life in order to follow their vision. Sickened, saddened, ridiculed, they decided to hold their own exhibition which was what formed the group. They were outlaws in the art world, accused of smearing and daubing, and needing to show their badly executed, unsaleable canvases privately – for who would hang such things? Instead of being garlanded, they were humiliated and despised. It was, however, a good time to buy – in 1878 you could pick up a Monet for 60 old francs, (which at that time was worth £2.35, $11.40) or a Renoir for 31F (£1.25, $5.90).

Being the creatures we are, each time we approach a painting we carry with us a portmanteau of what we have known in the past. We do it with everything – a mouthful of soufflé, the way no-one can sing *Every Time We Say Goodbye* like Ella, with conversations, with relationships. We can't help it, and we call it experience – probably a leftover from survival situations (this seems a friendly bear, let's compare him to that other bear who chewed my leg off). In paintings, we now know how to look at suggestions and whispers, but the nineteenth century public did not. Photography was releasing the painter from the function of recorder, and

*A little needlepoint picture inspired by Monet's atmospheric wild* Poppies, *painted at Argenteuil in 1873 – the movement of the waving grasses is achieved with long interwoven stitches.*

suddenly familiar benchmarks were torn away. A painting was no longer a disciplined world held within a frame. With the new realization that nature is neither composed nor symmetrical, that the effects of light and movement are transient, reality exploded with dizzying chaos. The Impressionists threw light, they dazzled eyes – and the viewer was shocked.

They painted snatches, moments, movements, fast fragments, flickering strokes, refracted prisms, paint leaping tumultuously on the canvas. They painted, and celebrated, the ordinary without romanticizing. The invention of the zinc tube meant colors could be easily transported, and the world outside the studio allowed them to record the fleeting effects of an atmosphere that changed constantly. They believed what they saw, with no need for a finished surface, nor one style of brushstroke. . . variety, vitality, immediacy was what mattered. Monet once said that he would like to have been born blind and then receive the gift of sight – he would have painted color without recognizing the objects. For him, it happened in reverse: with his eyesight failing, he saw only colors, luminosity, radiant neon auras. He painted what he saw, not what he knew to be there, and he let nothing interfere with the quivering energies of matter. Manet felt 'there is but one real thing, to put down at once what you see. When it's done, it's done'.

The book is divided into four sections: En Plein Air, Still Life, Gardens and The Face of Impressionism. There is some cross-pollination between the sections – for example, what began as a Renoir still life ended up as a needlepoint cushion in a poppy field in the Plein Air section; a shawl on a portrait became a hat and fell more comfortably into the Still Life section.

The book happened originally because of a love we both have for the period and the paintings, and we must acknowledge those who then joined the carousel: Ros Neale and her interpretative skills; Julie Baldwin on cushions; Ron Levin on frames; Cathy Sinker on inspiration and energy; Tim Imrie on cameras; Rostropovich on cello; Maggie Pearlstine on every form of encouragement in her repertoire; Djien, Sorel and Tamsin on charts; everyone at Ebury Press who made it happen; and the battery of wonderful friends who, on enquiring about health and progress, were told, 'Renoir is crippled with rheumatism, Berthe Morisot has just died – how can you ask such a question?!'

Mostly acknowledgments must go to that group of men and women who gave us such riches, when much in the way we live today seems designed to do the opposite. Thank you all. The light is always left on.

*Dramatic chair covered in needlepoint adapted from one of Monet's Giverny paintings of 1910 – following the brushstrokes produced this wonderfully free and spontaneous effect.*

# EN PLEIN AIR

'Everything that is painted directly on the spot always has a force, a power, a vivacity of touch that cannot be recreated in the studio'.

Eugène Boudin

The Impressionists were not the first to paint in the open air. Turner was said to have strapped himself to the mast of a ship in order to paint a storm, and over the years many artists painted outside, but by the 1860s it had become *de rigueur.* Pissarro encouraged his friends, Morisot encouraged Manet, but Monet was the most passionate – in his series of *Poplars* he worked on canvases in rotation, seven minutes was the longest he could spend on each before the sunlight moved from a certain leaf. Plein-airisme was a revelation to Monet, but his attitude to visual truth was thought excessive – after all, was not *style* considered everything?

On a trip to Honfleur, Monet argued with Bazille that an artist had no right to add to reality. They stayed at the Ferme St. Siméon and Monet was so poor he had to pay the *patronne* in drawings. The place is now upgraded, from simplicity to opulence, possibly on the proceeds of those same drawings. The view of the estuary they all loved now includes picturesque oil refineries – perhaps Monet would argue that an artist has every right to *subtract* from reality.

The idea of models posing outside – and given the same importance as trees and leaves – was new; the effect of air moving was new. It was technology that enabled them to paint completely from nature. Prior to the invention of tin tubes for paint, an artist travelled heavy, with pigs' bladders full of paint, pots of pigments, oils, grinders, as well as the other accoutrements of painting. Renoir said 'Without paint in tubes, there would have been no Cézanne, no Monet, no Sisley or Pissarro, nothing of what the journalists were later to call Impressionism . . .'

It was the philosophy of the moment, absorption in the exhilaration of movement, the fugitive effects of light, the analysis of shadows, the play of luminous colors that fascinated them – and all this was stronger outdoors. They believed their eyes, and their eyes alone, and ignored lessons from the past. In the separation of tone and the decomposition of light they were all alchemists. The desire was to capture something transient.

How precious their master classes would have been, if videoed for posterity. They left copious letters and some pieces of advice – both Pissarro and Monet, for example, recommended covering the canvas as quickly as possible to clarify the overall tone. Not very overwhelming is it, from such great masters? We think they'd have understood what comfort their own insecure words would have brought to insecure fellow painters, distant lessons, whispered camaraderie.

And there are authentic details of plein-airisme detectable on the canvas under magnification: grains of sand, leaf mold, a cheese sandwich.

*Previous page: needlepoint cushion adapted from Cézanne's glorious river scene, painted near Pontoise in 1877, imitating his great sweeps of color and rhythm with long diagonal stitches.*

*Our needlepoint picture on its frame was inspired by John Singer Sargent's* Claude Monet Painting at the Edge of a Wood, *painted in 1888.*

# SPRING FLOWERS

FROM *SPRING BOUQUET* BY PIERRE-AUGUST RENOIR

'The work of art must seize upon you, wrap you up in itself,
carry you away.'

At fifteen, Renoir became apprenticed to paint decorations on porcelain and this formed his basic training. *Spring Bouquet* was painted in 1866 when student days were finished – Renoir already knew Monet, Sisley, Pissarro and Cézanne; he had been rejected by the Salon. He painted this beautiful picture for the Le Coeur family. The flowers are marvellous – Renoir was seduced by the decorative effects he could achieve and already had one foot firmly pointed towards Impressionism. His genius was such that we not only see these suggestive petals, but can smell and feel them, convinced they have just been picked from hedge and garden and thrust gloriously, carefully, carelessly into a vase.

Renoir's life was long and his style evolved according to his changing circumstances, shifting sideways, taking new avenues. When he was young he created glorious paintings that show uniquely the romantic pleasures of Parisian life – his work is flooded with happiness, canvases where sunlight trembles and foliage shimmers, smiling shop girls and clerks dance in rhythmic polka afternoons, full of laughter.

Later came fatherhood, responsibility, poverty and sometimes depression – what we would today call a midlife crisis. He wrote 'I want to find what I am looking for before giving up.' He became provincial and isolated; the joy that had come so naturally now evaded him. At one point he returned to the traditions of eighteenth century techniques, feeling he no longer knew how to draw or paint. When he eventually achieved critical and financial success, his painting became optimistic again and the happiness we associate with him returned.

It was at the end of his life, too frail to move independently, paralysed by rheumatism, that somehow his great joie-de-vivre was miraculously channelled through his crippled hand and he created his most astonishingly luminous and sensual work. He painted flesh tinged hot with red and gold, extraordinary bodies like fruits ripening in the sun. Not everyone liked them. Mary Cassatt, never one to mince her words, wrote 'He is doing the most awful pictures of enormously fat red women.'

The two little panels based on Renoir's painting are deliberately simple, using just tent stitch. The picture frame was photographed on a hillside in intense summer heat while the air vibrated with the sound of insects. Wild poppies were everywhere, scatterings of dog roses; little mouthfuls of the world that have as much right to be celebrated as large miracles – something Renoir felt very strongly.

*Previous page: a gentle needlepoint picture, taken from Berthe Morisot's beautiful study, painted at Bougival in 1882, of a child offering a posy of wild flowers to her mother.*

## STITCHING DETAILS

Finished size of design:
Each panel measures 9 x 32.5cm (3½ x 12¾in)

Yarn colors and quantities

| DMC Laine Zephyr | | | Skeins |
|---|---|---|---|
| | 746 | Cream | 2 |
| | 755 | Pink | 1 |
| | 842 | Mushroom | 3 |
| | 3078 | Yellow | 2 |
| | 436 | Honey | 2 |
| | 928 | Gray-blue | 3 |
| | 932 | Petrol blue | 2 |
| | 3349 | Apple green | 4 |
| | 940 | Leaf green | 3 |
| | 3345 | Dark green | 4 |
| | 415 | Light gray | 3 |
| | 317 | Dark gray | 3 |
| | 100 | White | 2 |

### Canvas

14-gauge white mono deluxe
Size: 31 x 41cm (12 x 16in)

### Other materials

Tapestry needle, size 20
Ruler or tape measure
Masking tape for binding the canvas
Sharp scissors for cutting the canvas
Embroidery scissors
Sharp HB pencil or fine permanent marker in suitable color
Eraser

Before beginning to stitch, please read the general information on page 138.

## Marking the canvas and following the chart

Cut the canvas to size and bind the edges with masking tape. The design does not have to be marked on the canvas; just follow the chart opposite. The squares represent the canvas intersections, not the holes. Each square represents one tent stitch. The chart is divided into units of 10 squares by 10 squares to make it easier to follow. Before beginning to stitch, it may be helpful to mark out your canvas in similar units of 10 squares by 10 squares with an HB pencil or permanent marker. Mark the top of the canvas so that, if you turn the canvas while stitching, you will still know where the top is.

## Stitches used

TENT stitch (1) is used throughout. For stitch instructions, see page 140.

## Stitching the design

Use the whole thread of Zephyr wool (4 strands) throughout. It might be easiest to start at the top right-hand corner, 4–5cm (1½–2in) in from the corner, working horizontally from one block of color to another.

## Making up instructions

The needlepoint may need to be stretched back into shape (see page 138). Then make it up into a cushion (see page 143). The panels could also be framed individually. Use a professional framer who will also stretch them for you.

*Overleaf: inspired by the work of Eugène Boudin, whose observant and informal beach-scenes at resorts like Trouville greatly appealed to the Impressionists.*

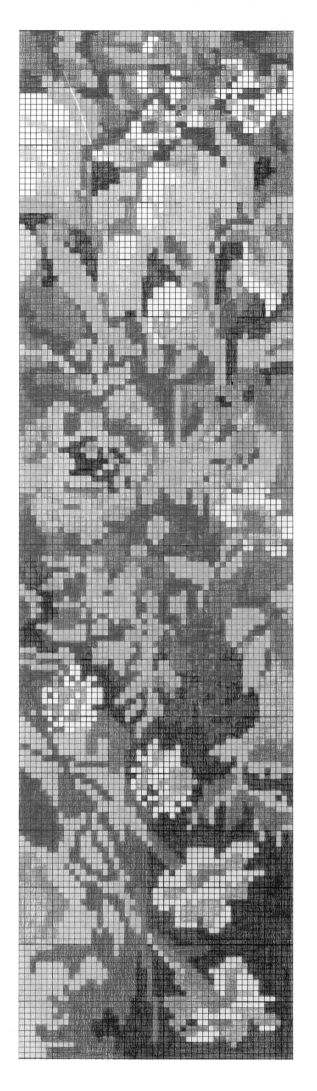

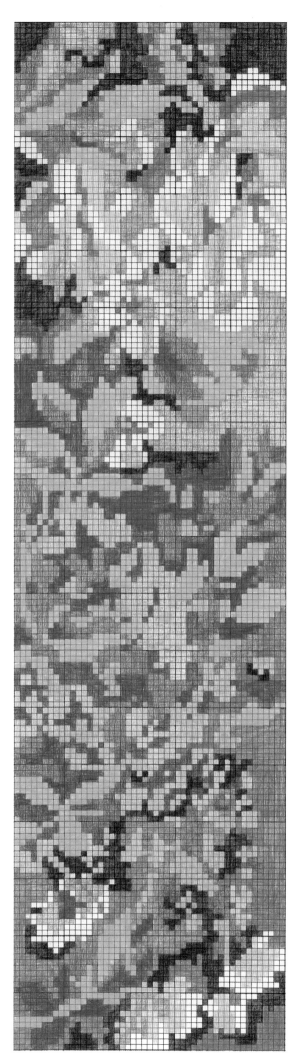

# THE SEINE AT MARLY
## BY CAMILLE PISSARRO

'Remember that I have the temperament of a peasant, I am melancholy, harsh and savage in my works, it is only in the long run that I can expect to please, provided those who look at my pictures have a grain of indulgence.

But the eye of the passer-by is too hasty and sees only the surface.'

Pissarro – daddy of the Impressionists, philosopher of the group, always questioning, experimenting, anarchic, inspiring, literate . . . the indelible picture of him is at his kitchen table after a meal of perhaps potato soup and bread, giving his many children drawing lessons, instilling and repeating 'do not neglect nature'. He struggled, with himself, with his creativity, with poverty. It wasn't until he was in his sixties that he had financial security, managing to buy a house and finally achieve some serenity, painting in that last decade some of his most joyous scenes of Parisian life ('while struggling against old age', he wrote to Monet).

There is something low-key about Pissarro, an 'egg' man, rather than a 'soufflé' man. His work is pitched modestly, no flamboyant gestures, rural paintings with a beautiful earthy quality. He gives the impression of a single-minded commitment: his orchards, streets, country scenes are so intense, so simple, you feel his feet planted in the soil. Day after day, trudging out with easel, umbrella and canvas on his back, numbed by the winter cold, driven by the intangible and unquenchable. If the creativity tap is turned, the flow can trickle or gush, with necessity, passion,

dissatisfaction; the safety valve of the overflow doesn't always operate, the process between eye and hand becomes unstoppable. Pissarro's subjects may be simple, but the hand that holds the brush is like iron.

At the outbreak of the Franco-Prussian war in 1870, Pissarro, like Monet, came to London to paint. On his return to France he discovered that his house had been occupied by the Prussians, and that out of 1,500 paintings stored there, only about 40 remained undamaged. Any Pissarro exhibition will have this tragic gap in it.

*The Seine at Marly* was painted just after his return, with no suggestion of recent events – are the trees ravaged, is there an atmosphere of sadness? No, the painter managed to paint only what he saw, separating emotion from canvas . . . the couple continue to stroll in the idyllic afternoon.

Autumn is the season most dominated by the passage of time, a transition between summer's last throes and winter's paralysis. Autumn sounds so noisy and smells so strong, of mold and woodsmoke. On days reflected gold, when breath vaporizes and the sky is washed and cantering, the leaves combust in plum and amber, simmering, shimmering, and you know the only explanation is that the Universal Impressionist has been flinging his palette of ochers and siennas at the trees . . . and how wonderful that he does. Pissarro painted *The Seine at Marly* on such a day.

We have taken a section of this beautiful painting and worked it very simply, breaking Pissarro's colors down into patchworks of shades, mixing the yarn in a few places to suggest the softness of shadow. The picture is worked entirely in tent stitch. If you prefer, the figures can be highlighted as we have shown, using the simple stitches described.

### Marking the canvas and following the chart

Cut the canvas to size and bind the edges with masking tape. The design does not have to be marked out on the canvas; just follow the color chart on page 28. Remember that the squares represent the canvas intersections, not the holes. Each square represents one tent stitch.

The chart is divided into units of 10 squares by 10 squares to make it easier to follow. Before beginning to stitch, it may be helpful to mark out your canvas in similar units of 10 squares by 10 squares with an HB pencil or permanent marker. We suggest marking the top of the canvas so that, if you turn the canvas while stitching, you will still know where the top is.

### Stitches used

TENT stitch (1)
Optional:
Diagonal SATIN stitch (2), Vertical BRICK stitch (4) over two threads, STEM stitch (7). For stitch instructions see page 140.

### Stitching the design

The whole thread of Zephyr wool (4 strands) has been used throughout. The wool has been mixed in certain areas and this is indicated on the color key. Where it is mixed, use two strands of each color. An explanation on how to split the wool appears on page 139.

Begin in any area you wish. It might be easiest to start at the top right-hand corner, 4–5cm (1½–2in) in from the corner, working horizontally from one block of color to another. If you intend to use stitchery for part of the design, work it after the TENT stitch (1).

You can sew the whole design in TENT stitch (1) throughout. Alternatively, you can work certain areas of the design in stitchery to give an added dimension to the two figures. Refer to the color photograph of the framed picture for the direction and position of the stitches. If you decide to

## STITCHING DETAILS

Finished size of design:
19 x 39.5 cm (7½ x 15⅛in)

Yarn colors and quantities

| | DMC Laine Zephyr | | Skeins |
|---|---|---|---|
| | 746 | Cream | 3 |
| | 762 | Sky blue | 1 |
| | 676 | Yellow | 3 |
| | 832 | Yellow ocher | 2 |
| | 360 | Salmon pink | 3 |
| | 351 | Flamingo | 1 |
| | 350 | Flame red | 1 |
| | 632 | Marron | 1 |
| | 644 | Beige | 2 |
| | 3042 | Mauve | 2 |
| | 523 | Ash green | 3 |
| | 522 | Green | 3 |
| | 319 | Bottle green | 2 |
| | 802 | Turquoise | 2 |
| | 560 | Kingfisher | 3 |
| | 451 | Gray | 3 |
| | 413 | Charcoal | 4 |
| | 372 | Sap green | 3 |
| | 612 | Brown | 2 |

Mixed colors

| | |
|---|---|
| | 832/3042 |
| | 3042/372 |
| | 413/451 |
| | 676/360 |

### Canvas

14-gauge white deluxe
Size: 30.5 x 48cm (12 x 19in)

### Other materials

Tapestry needle, size 20
Ruler or tape measure
Masking tape for binding the canvas
Sharp scissors for cutting the canvas
Embroidery scissors
Sharp HB pencil or fine permanent marker in suitable color
Eraser

Before beginning to stitch, please read the general information on page 138.

use stitchery, leave this until the end.

We have stitched the lady's jacket and skirt in vertical BRICK stitch (4) over two threads; the man's trousers are in TENT stitch (1). Their hats are stitched in diagonal SATIN stitch (2) with outlining where indicated in STEM stitch (7).

## Making up instructions

When the design has been sewn, the needlepoint may need to be stretched back into shape (see stretching instructions on page 138). You may prefer to take your needlepoint to a professional picture framer who will also stretch it.

# MISTY MORNING

## BY ALFRED SISLEY

'I must give something to my butcher and my grocer; to one I have paid nothing for six months and to the other nothing for a year.'

Sisley was born in Paris of English parents and, at eighteen, was sent to London to follow a business career. After four years he abandoned the attempt and returned to Paris. He began studying painting at Gleyre's studio and met Monet, Renoir and Bazille. For some years his father supported him, during which time his landscapes were heavy and somber, influenced by past masters. In 1870 paternal sponsorship stopped due to business failure and coincidentally Sisley's colors brightened, he became more daring and his talent began to blossom (could it have been lightheadedness induced by hunger?).

Sisley is considered an Impressionist in the truest sense, always faithful to landscape painting, and apparently not tempted to wander down the experimental avenues that beckoned the others. A lifetime of painting with fresh, spontaneous eyes can be hard to sustain, particularly with the corrosive struggles of ill health and poverty. There is something melancholy about his work, a quiet voice within blinkered scenes. To paint nature as he did, the heart, as well as eye and mind, is open and attuned, and in such a state of trust, harshness of daily life can be abrasive to someone so sensitive. Is there a universal well of sadness that can be slipped into unsuspectingly? Poor Sisley, even on his deathbed, when one hopes for some serene evaluation, he was worried about doctors' bills.

## STITCHING DETAILS

Finished size of design:
40 x 32 cm (16 x 12½in)

Yarn colors and quantities

| DMC Laine Zephyr | | | Skeins |
|---|---|---|---|
| · | 373 | Aqua | 6 |
| | 828 | Turquoise blue | 3 |
| | 813 | Bright blue | 1 |
| | 933 | Dull blue | 5 |
| | 929 | Airforce blue | 4 |
| | 452 | Taupe | 4 |
| | 523 | Ash green | 3 |
| | 843 | Beige | 9 |
| | 772 | Lime green | 1 |
| | 369 | Almond green | 1 |
| | 3047 | Lemon | 1 |
| | 676 | Bright yellow | 1 |
| · | 226 | Dusky pink | 3 |
| | 818 | Sugar pink | 1 |
| | 756 | Rose pink | 1 |
| | 317 | Slate gray | 2 |

### Mixed colors

| | |
|---|---|
| | 638 Cream (1 skein)/373 |
| | 373/843 |
| | 373/226 |

### Canvas

12-gauge white deluxe
Size: 45 x 37cm (18 x 14½in)

### Other materials

Tapestry needle, size 18 or 20
Ruler or tape measure
Masking tape for binding the canvas
Sharp scissors for cutting the canvas
Embroidery scissors
Sharp HB pencil or fine permanent marker in
suitable color
Eraser

Before beginning to stitch, please read the
general information on page 138.

*Misty Morning* is our favorite Sisley painting; it is marvellously atmospheric, creating beautiful vaporous illusions. It is the end of autumn, there is hoar frost, the brittle petals of the chrysanthemums are about to snap, an old woman gathers the last of the herbs into her apron. The sun will soon dispel the mist that tantalizes the viewer, and the taste of winter approaches. His brushwork is so free, scribbling paint across the surface, barely there, an insinuation of sky, a shrug of tree. So fast, so exquisite. Sisley did this painting soon after he discarded his heavy colors, in the years when he was as hungry as Renoir or Monet. In fact the three were good friends, and passers-by would stare at their unusual long-haired appearance. Could he have imagined, and would it have helped him to know, that one day *Misty Morning* would be worth an unthinkable sum, and hang in one of the world's great museums?

To try to create a similar look in wool was interesting. The colors, already muted, were mixed together to make them almost indefinable. Only tent stitch was used to give a deliberately flat appearance – close up everything is subtle, it is only from a distance that the shapes appear.

## Marking the canvas and following the chart

Cut the canvas to size and bind the edges with masking tape. The design does not have to be marked out on the canvas; just follow the color chart on page 33. Remember that the squares represent the canvas intersections, not the holes. Each square represents one tent stitch. The chart is divided into units of 10 squares by 10 squares to make it easier to follow. Before stitching, it may be helpful to mark your canvas in similar units of 10 squares with an HB pencil or permanent marker. Mark the top of the canvas so that, if you turn the canvas while stitching, you will still know where the top is.

## Stitches used

TENT stitch (1), Reversed TENT stitch (1a) ◹ .

## Stitching the design

The whole thread of Zephyr wool (4 strands) has been used throughout. The wool has been mixed in certain areas and this is indicated on the color key. Where it is mixed, use 2 strands of each color. An explanation on how to split the wool appears on page 139. Begin in any area you wish. It might be easiest to start at the top right-hand corner, 4–5cm (1½–2in) in from the corner, working horizontally from one block of color to another.

## Finishing and making up

We feel that a needlepoint picture should be stretched and framed by a professional.

# PARIS, A RAINY DAY

## BY GUSTAVE CAILLEBOTTE

'A painter's truest arguments are his paintings, and however right he may be in all he says, he is at his truest in his work.'

Gustave Caillebotte was inestimably important to the Impressionists individually and to the movement as a whole. He was extremely gifted, painting powerful images from unexpected viewpoints, his work challenging convention as excitingly as any of his fellow Impressionists. There are two versions of *A Rainy Day*, the first, painted in 1876, was realistically polished to a traditional finish, the second, shown here, painted at almost the same time: loose, alive and full of movement. There is such a feeling of Paris, its cobbles and boulevards, the sensation of that elegant epoch, shown from a standpoint at rue de St Petersbourg and Place de Clichy.

Caillebotte was a naval architect, yachtsman and also a passionate gardener – he may well have ignited Monet with his enthusiasm for flower growing. He was very wealthy, and during the years of non-recognition helped those in the group who were struggling – he bought their paintings at inflated prices, gave them gifts, and, according to one story, bought back his own paintings at auction to raise money for a group exhibition.

Caillebotte's paintings are less known than his spectacular legacy. He had a premonition of an early death and in his will bequeathed his collection of Impressionist paintings to the state. He died at forty-six, and, with Renoir acting as executor and not without controversy, the paintings of Monet, Renoir, Manet, Degas, Pissarro, Sisley and Cézanne and his own marvellous *Floor Strippers*, a total of sixty paintings, were eventually given to the nation – the majority becoming the core of France's Impressionist collection.

The Musée d'Orsay, where they are now housed, is impressive, comfortable, conducive to observing. But can anything compare to the first-sight of Impressionists in their old home, the Jeu de Paume? We are line-refusers, show us a line and we go into a 'non, merci' routine, but in the past not only have we queued there without question but even felt privileged to be doing so.

In those days, a visit to the crowded Jeu de Paume was an orgasmic bombardment, such riches squeezed and cramped in corners, behind doors, up stairs; it was too overwhelming. Imagine an overcrowded party staged by Zeffirelli, every guest the Dalai Lama dressed by Lacroix, the air perfumed with black truffles and vintage armagnac . . . the energy of all those paintings in one place was enough to make the roof come off. The Musée d'Orsay's respectful airiness can't compare – we have never yet left there stunned and spinning, whereas the Jeu de Paume did that every time.

Perhaps it was the lack of oxygen.

The needlepoint is worked in a mixture of wool, stranded cotton and coton perlé, all to add sparkle and texture, in restrained colors, using stitchery for emphasis.

## Marking the canvas

This is a combined chart and artwork design. Trace the outline (from pages 146–7) and follow the 'Marking the canvas' instructions on page 94.

## Stitches used

TENT stitch (1), BRICK stitch (over two threads) (4), STEM stitch (7).

## Stitching the People and the Umbrella

Use the whole thread of Zephyr wool (4 strands), the whole thread (6 strands) of Coton Mouliné Spécial and the whole thread of Coton Perlé throughout with one exception: for all *outlining* in either Coton Mouliné Spécial or Zephyr wool, use 2 strands. An explanation for splitting the wool appears on page 139.

The wool has been mixed on the faces and this is indicated on the color key. Where it is mixed, use 2 strands of each color.

The instructions on page 140 will show you how to work the stitches. The numbers on the colored artwork refer to the stitch numbers. Look at the photograph of the made up picture and the colored artwork to show you which color goes where (the arrows show the direction of the stitches). Remember, this is a guide, do not be restricted by it and feel free to experiment.

Begin by stitching the two people followed by the umbrella. The clothes and hats are stitched in BRICK stitch (4) over two threads edged in STEM stitch (7). His shirt and their hands and faces are worked in TENT stitch (1), edged in STEM stitch (7). The handle of the umbrella is worked in two rows of STEM stitch (7). The umbrella is in TENT stitch (1) and edged in STEM stitch (7).

## Following the chart

When you have completed stitching the people, follow the color chart and 'fill in' the background. The squares represent the canvas intersections, not the holes. Each square represents one TENT stitch. The chart is divided into units of 10 squares by 10 squares to make it easier to follow. Before beginning to stitch the background, it may be helpful to mark out your canvas in similar units of 10 squares by 10 squares with an HB pencil or permanent marker.

To enable you to differentiate between cream and white, we have used a

## STITCHING DETAILS

Finished size of design:
29 x 41cm (11½ x 16in)

Yarn colors and quantities

| | DMC Coton Perlé No 3 | | Skeins |
|---|---|---|---|
| • | 712 | Cream | 3 |
| | 745 | Yellow | 2 |
| | 945 | Peach | 2 |
| | 948 | Shell pink | 2 |
| | Blanc | White | 2 |

| | DMC Laine Zephyr | | Skeins |
|---|---|---|---|
| | 3043 | Orchid | 2 |
| | 762 | Pale blue | 2 |
| | 928 | Eau de nil | 2 |
| | 632 | Terracotta | 3 |
| | 524 | Almond | 2 |
| | 3032 | Beige | 2 |
| | 452 | Pale elephant | 3 |
| | 451 | Dark elephant | 1 |
| | 415 | Pale gray | 3 |
| | 414 | Mid-gray | 4 |
| | 317 | Dark gray | 5 |
| | 348 | Black | 4 |
| | 950 | Peach | 2 |

### Mixed colors

| | | |
|---|---|---|
| • | 950/632 | |

| | DMC Coton Mouliné Spécial | | Skeins |
|---|---|---|---|
| | 3042 | Heather | 2 |

### Canvas

14-gauge white interlock
Size: 40 x 51cm (15½ x 20in)

### Other materials

Tapestry needle, size 20
Ruler or tape measure
Masking tape for binding the canvas
Sharp scissors for cutting the canvas
Embroidery scissors
Sharp HB pencil or fine permanent marker in
suitable color
Eraser

Before beginning to stitch, please read the
general information on page 138.

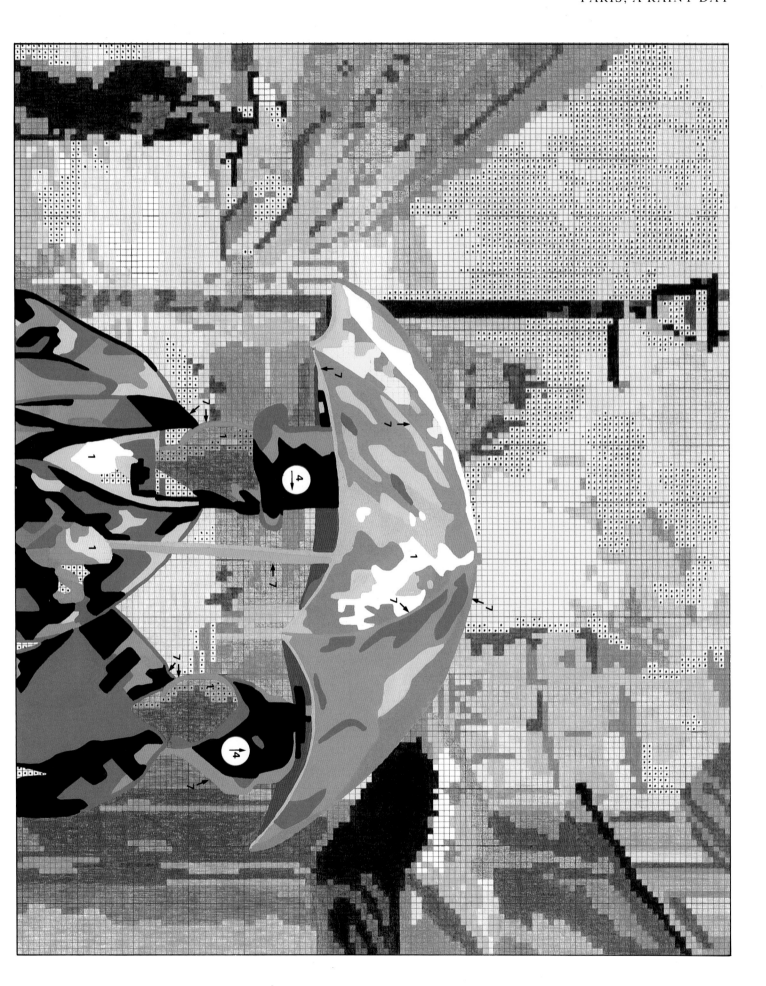

black dot for the cream areas. Where there is no dot, white yarn has been used – see color key. The corresponding yarns are given in the color key.

### Stitching the background

The background is worked entirely in TENT stitch (1). Begin in any area you wish. It might be easiest to start by 'filling in' the stitches on the edge of the figures and work outwards. Do not be concerned if you have to compensate by leaving out some stitches as everyone will trace and stitch the outline of the people in a slightly different way.

### Finishing and making up

Many needlepointers feel experienced enough to stretch and make up their needlework designs into cushions, but we always feel that a needlepoint picture should be stretched and framed by a professional.

# SNOWSCENE

FROM *THE MAGPIE* BY CLAUDE MONET

'It is so difficult, so fragile and delicate, and I tend to be so brutal.'

The snowscene was painted in 1869, a very bad year for Monet. His work was sometimes halted by lack of money for paints, he didn't eat every day, and relied on Renoir to bring bread for his wife Camille and son Jean. Renoir was in a similar position, doing little work because he didn't have many paints, but didn't have the despairing temperament that once made Monet throw himself into a river.

Monet's work had been refused by the official Salon jury – the establishment figures felt that the group were a 'bunch of mad men' and declared it their duty to stop the paintings being seen. His family would not help financially, and he lived from hand to mouth, borrowing money wherever possible. In August of 1869 he wrote to Bazille, another of the group, asking for more money: 'For a week no bread, no wine, no fire for cooking, no light. It's terrible. . .'

We wanted to include a snowscene in this book. It is such a difficult subject to paint, giving form to the formless, a portrait without cheekbones, the Pillsbury dough man. Such genius: to convey snow you can smell – just to stand in front of such a painting makes the air thinner, the nostrils contract. Perhaps we are so fascinated by snow because in Britain it's such an occasion. No-one ever expects it – like rain, when the roads flood; heatwaves, when the roads melt; Autumn when leaves disrupt trains and block drains – these things always take the British by surprise. This legacy means that most of us still get that leap of excitement when we look outside

one morning and see every tree branch balancing a slice of meringue. We walk with adult dignity, but we are not all still children longing to shake the snow from overhead boughs, stuff balls of it into boot-tops, lick it from a companion's upturned face?

There are many Impressionist snowscenes. Renoir called them the leprosy of nature. For us there was a shortlist of one. Monet's *Magpie* has no grayness in it, only radiance, and he has confronted this glittering scene head-on. The painting could have the caption: face the sun and the shadows will always fall behind you. The painting is glorious: the midwinter sun is setting early (your feet are starting to get numb), the shadows are long and blue, the snow will soon crystallize and drop percussion-like from the hedges. The needlepoint has been worked in simple tent stitch, mixing the color on the sky to achive a blending of tones. For some branches we have used stem stitch to help them keep their spindly silhouettes. The Snowscene is shown here as a cushion – it also looks excellent as a picture, mounted in an elaborate gold frame.

### Marking the canvas and following the chart

Cut the canvas to size and bind the edges with masking tape. The design does not have to be marked out on the canvas; just follow the color chart on page 44. Remember that the squares represent the canvas intersections, not the holes. Each square represents one tent stitch.

The chart is divided into units of 10 squares by 10 squares to make it easier to follow. Before beginning to stitch, it may be helpful to mark out your canvas in similar units of 10 squares by 10 squares with an HB pencil or permanent marker in a suitable color. Also, we suggest marking the top of the canvas so that, if you turn the canvas while stitching, you will still know where the top is.

### Stitches used

TENT stitch (1), Reversed TENT stitch (1a) ◻, STEM stitch (7). For the stitch instructions see page 140.

### Stitching the design

Use the whole thread of Zephyr wool (4 strands) throughout. We have mixed the wool in certain areas and this is indicated on the color key. Where it is mixed, use 2 strands of each color. Begin with TENT stitch (1) in any area you wish. It might be easiest to start at the top right-hand corner, 4–5cm (1½–2in) in from the corner, working horizontally from one block of color to another.

Reversed TENT stitch (1a) has been used in certain areas and this is indicated on the chart.

We have used STEM stitch (7) to outline the magpie, the gate, the top of the hedge and the branches – see the color chart and the photograph of the made-up cushion for the position. If you find there are spaces once you have worked the STEM stitch (7), 'fill in' with TENT stitches (1) in the relevant colors.

### Making up instructions

When the design has been sewn, the needlepoint may need to be stretched back into shape (see stretching instructions on page 138). Then make it up into a cushion as shown on page 142.

## STITCHING DETAILS

Finished size of design:
47 x 33cm (18½ x 13in)

Yarn colors and quantities

| | DMC Laine Zephyr | | Skeins |
|---|---|---|---|
| | 100 | White | 1 |
| | 746 | Cream | 10 |
| | 3078 | Yellow | 5 |
| | 773 | Pale green | 8 |
| | 3072 | Pale jade | 5 |
| | 523 | Gray-green | 4 |
| | 802 | Turquoise | 3 |
| | 928 | Pale airforce blue | 6 |
| | 929 | Airforce blue | 3 |
| | 372 | Pale olive | 3 |
| | 762 | Pale sky blue | 3 |
| | 799 | Sky blue | 3 |
| | 640 | Donkey brown | 2 |
| | 3030 | Milk chocolate | 2 |
| | 451 | Gray | 3 |
| | 934 | Dark olive | 5 |

### Mixed colors

| | |
|---|---|
| • | 773/762 |

### Canvas

14-gauge white mono deluxe
Size: 57 x 43cm (22½ x 17in)

### Other materials

Tapestry needle, size 20
Ruler or tape measure
Masking tape for binding the canvas
Sharp scissors for cutting the canvas
Embroidery scissors
Sharp HB pencil or fine permanent marker in
suitable color
Eraser

Before beginning to stitch, please read the
general information on page 138.

STILL LIFE

Still life, life suspended – not what we experience every day in traffic jams and checkout lines, but a group of objects, carefully placed. It gives artists something to paint when there is no money for a model, and the weather too bad to paint outside – a baguette on the table, some apples, a piece of fish, today's lunch, tomorrow's breakfast.

Following Cézanne's example, still life developed further. Portraits became still life, flesh exposed as on an operating slab, the surgeon wielding a cruel paintbrush. A still life composition is complete, it doesn't encourage us to ask what came before or after (unless the pheasant is so high we wait for it to crawl off the table on its own).

We are all still life artists in one form or another – whether arranging jam jars and cereal boxes on the breakfast table, or blotter, jotter, pens in order of height; even creeping downstairs in the night to rearrange the videos into pleasing stacks. We have a wonderful girlfriend who cannot pass a shelf without regrouping it – stand still long enough and she will regroup your collar, sleeves, eyebrows. Her bedroom is a still life in shades of white – porcelain pieces, fragrant Victorian sachets, antique lace and silver. We swear the bedcover is ironed daily before the groups of fragile, frilled pillows are arranged on it. The man in her life has learned to sleep without disturbing the composition.

The French quaintly call the subject dead nature, and it is the discipline that most new painters progress to after 'Palm Tree Silhouetted against Sunset'. In art institutes all over the world, tables are spread with earthenware jugs and sprouting onions, aspirations are attempted and perhaps fulfilled, before statues and skulls, grapes and drapes are added.

There is enormous skill in making such an arrangement. It may even be inborn. The great masters of our own era are often aged between 12 and 21, creating private gems out of a sneaker, an antique peanut butter sandwich, unthreaded beads, an unravelled cassette. The classical version of this includes a paperback of Homer's *Odyssey*. Bathroom arrangements can be even better: toiletries dribbling from unscrewed lids, a lone sock, a cottonwool bud, your best needlework scissors, the whole nestling on the dog's towel under the radiator, like some primeval swamp. A true expert, once the 'vignette' has been mastered, will go on to the Still Life room. Here the phrase 'Dead Nature' really comes into its own, as the genre relies heavily on plates of abandoned food. This is the Nuclear Warhead Still Life and is created not by adding objects, but by the appearance of an explosion from within. You will often see as the centerpiece of such an arrangement, the artist itself sadly looking for a pair of knickers.

Living with such instinctive interior decorators is a handicap if you are trying to sell your house. It means tiptoeing past the closed door and whispering, 'I'm so sorry, you can't look in there, my child is ill.'

*Previous page: tasselled hats and belts, using rich patterns as painted by Manet, Monet and Monticelli. They interpreted fabric designs onto canvas – we turned them back to fabric in needlepoint.*

*Monet painted this still life of paintbox and palette,* The Corner of a Studio, *1861 – the rich classic colors adapted beautifully to a bookcover.*

# A POSY OF VIOLETS

Violets are a recurring Impressionist theme. Manet painted Morisot holding a bunch of violets – she eventually bought the painting herself and it still hangs in her Paris home. In the same year he painted a small posy picture, *Bunch of Violets*, shown on the right, dedicated to her, his beautiful muse.

Violets have been cultivated for over 2,000 years for their scent and color, but not content with being overwhelmed by that, we also crystallize and eat them. Shakespeare still knows a bank whereon the nodding violet grows, and on another river bank they were first seen where Orpheus slept. Violets were favoured by Elizabeth 1 and Napoleon, perhaps because they symbolize humility. In Manet's portrait, Morisot's posy gives her a Victorian air of reserve and shyness, which doesn't sit very comfortably with the image we have of her.

Violets have an ephemeral quality, with folded petals like colored origami tissue, hues so lovely a name was invented for them. There is something nostalgic about a dying posy of violets. It fades so discreetly, echoing a languid faltering of the hand, a first dance coyness, a shrinking violet. Frail dowagers with papery faces have violet bath salts in bowls with crystal lids, and a velvet posy with unravelling stems pinned to a lapel. We have a collection of tiny violet pieces – the perfume bottle still has its scent after several generations.

Enter the imaginary Violet de Brecourt. Her bureau is shown in the photograph. She has just returned from a carriage ride with Lucien, her lover, the confined interior making their proximity hard to bear. The Duc, her husband, has threatened Lucien's military career and will take away her children (who are only a little younger than Lucien himself) unless the liaison is ended. In despair, she returns to her room, drops her bag on the desk and fingers the namesake objects she loves as if for the last time. There seems no alternative. She begins to write: Mon cher Lucien. . . her hand falters. Where would the au pair have put the strychnine?

The starting point for Violet's bag was the beautiful silver frame and clasp. The background was worked in silver metal thread, a yarn with a mind of its own. However, the effect is marvellous, it has the heavy look of chainmail, and, as we all wanted to make ourselves waistcoats, jackets, armor out of it, we definitely feel that the effect is worth the effort. Alternatively, silver gray stranded cotton would look excellent.

We have worked the bag in tent stitch throughout, to look traditional and to be more practical – such tiny stitches are unlikely to catch. The back is plain silver. The violets could also be appliqued onto a jacket pocket or lace pillow, or worked on a larger gauge canvas for a cushion or footstool. They would look stunning on a dark green background.

## Marking the canvas and following the chart

Cut the canvas to size and bind the edges with masking tape. The design does not have to be marked out on the canvas; just follow the color chart opposite. Remember that the squares represent the canvas intersections, not the holes. Each square represents one TENT stitch.

The chart is divided into units of 10 squares by 10 squares to make it easier to follow. Before beginning to stitch, it may be helpful to mark out your canvas in similar units of 10 squares by 10 squares with an HB pencil or permanent marker in a suitable color. Also, we suggest marking the top of the canvas so that, if you turn the canvas while stitching, you will still know where the top is.

The background of the bag is worked in silver thread, shown white on the color chart.

## STITCHING DETAILS

Finished size of design:
18 x 19cm (7 x 7½in)

The design only appears on one side of the bag. The other side has been worked using silver thread alone and the quantities given include **both sides**.

We have used an antique handle attached to a dilapidated bag found in an antique shop. A pattern was made of the bag and the design worked according to the original shape. If you decide to do the same, you can adapt the design adding more background if you wish, or using less depending on the bag you purchase. A whole spool, with the thread worked double, sews approximately 65 sq cm (10 sq in) in TENT stitch.

Yarn colors and quantities

| | DMC Coton Mouliné Spécial | | Skeins |
|---|---|---|---|
| | 3721 | Rust | 1 |
| | 3743 | Pale violet | 1 |
| | 3042 | Mid violet | 1 |
| | 209 | Lavender | 2 |
| | 327 | Purple | 2 |
| | 550 | Dark mauve | 1 |
| | 825 | Peacock | 1 |
| | 3348 | Pale leaf green | 1 |
| | 3347 | Mid leaf green | 1 |
| | 3345 | Dark leaf green | 1 |
| | Blanc | White | 1 |
| | DMC Fil or clair (gold thread) | | 1 spool |
| | DMC Fil argent clair (silver thread) | | 7 spools |

### Canvas

18-gauge white mono deluxe
Size: 28 x 29cm (11 x 11½in)

### Other materials

Tapestry needle, size 22
Ruler or tape measure
Masking tape for binding the canvas
Sharp scissors for cutting the canvas
Embroidery scissors
Sharp HB pencil or fine permanent marker in suitable color
Eraser

Before beginning to stitch, please read the general information on page 138.

### Stitches used

TENT stitch (1) is used throughout. For the stitch instructions see page 140.

### Stitching the design

The whole thread (6 strands) of Coton Mouliné Spécial has been used throughout and 2 strands of metallic thread have been used for the background.

Begin in any area you wish. It might be easiest to start at the top right-hand corner, 4–5cm (1½–2in) in from the corner, working horizontally from one block of color to another.

### Making up instructions

This design will need to be stretched before making up into a bag – see stretching instructions on page 138. If you follow our idea and make it into a bag using an antique frame, you can use the original bag as a pattern when putting it together. Alternatively, you could make a cushion or a miniature picture.

# FANS

## BY EDOUARD MANET

'When I go out, I take lots of mandarins, I fill my pockets with them and give them to the local children who come begging. They'd probably prefer money, but I prefer to give them a share in something I enjoy!'

They all painted fans . . . the Spanish influence, the Japanese influence, and, when times were very bad, they even painted them to be mounted on sticks and sold as fans. Oriental goods started arriving in Paris in the 1860s. The impact of Japanese art on the Impressionists was significant, reinforcing their own breakthroughs with composition, things we now take for granted: altered viewpoints, devices to lead the eye into the picture, asymmetric use of space, the severing of a figure in close-up, the lowering and finally the elimination of horizons. Decorative elements crept into backgrounds, on to robes, shawls, kimonos, prints and the ubiquitous fans.

In needlepoint, we have been drawn to this Japanese influence over the years, from large wall-hangings to tiny bookmarks. The simplicity of the prints with their flowing outlines is excellent for canvas or linen, giving patchworks of areas to fill with interesting stitches – one of our favorite kits made for the Royal Academy of Arts was Falling Fans, for the Great Japan Exhibition.

Our Fans cushion came from Manet's *Lady with Fans* – a glorious portrait of Nina de Callias with a gold-leafed Japanese screen mounted on the wall behind her. We have taken a section of the screen to make into this rich cushion. Actually, we hated confining the needlepoint to a cushion. It would make a beautiful wall-hanging, or bed-head, or upholstery for a chaise-

longue or, or , or . . . There is something deliciously opulent about gold thread, gold tassels, gold frames; and it has a quite magical effect on embroidery.

Manet painted the picture in 1873, the year of his first  wholehearted acceptance at the official Salon, and also a period where his work was closest to what we recognize as Impressionism (though it's unfair to confine him to a label). Compare this success to the furore when he showed Olympia at the 1865 Salon – it made him so notorious he was derided as the figurehead of the Impressionist group of madmen, the worst insult possible.

## STITCHING DETAILS

Finished size of design:
35 x 35cm (13½ x 13½in)

Yarn colors and quantities

| DMC Laine Zephyr | | | Skeins |
|---|---|---|---|
| | 200 | Cream | 2 |
| | 402 | Orange | 2 |
| | 358 | Pale terracotta | 3 |
| | 356 | Dark terracotta | 1 |
| | 406 | Brown | 2 |
| | 436 | Ocher | 1 |
| | 640 | Taupe | 7 |
| | 3052 | Olive green | 3 |
| | 828 | Pale blue | 2 |
| | 802 | Turquoise | 1 |
| | 931 | Kingfisher | 1 |
| | 368 | Pale green | 1 |
| | 522 | Ash green | 4 |
| | 3363 | Dark green | 1 |
| | 317 | Gray | 2 |
| | 348 | Black | 5 |
| | | DMC Fil or clair (gold thread) | 3 spools |

### Canvas

12-gauge white mono deluxe
Size: 39 x 39cm (15½ x 15½in)

### Other materials

Tapestry needle, size 18 or 20
Ruler or tape measure
Masking tape for binding the canvas
Sharp scissors for cutting the canvas
Embroidery scissors
Sharp HB pencil or fine permanent marker in suitable color
Eraser

The painting hangs in the Musée d'Orsay, coolly, on high-tec walls, flanked quietly by other gilt-framed goodies . . . a far cry from how his paintings made their Salon debut: with thousands of others, frame to frame, floor to ceiling, crammed under 'M'. We knew the painting from reproductions, and one day we joined the queue, intending to make a single-minded bee-line for the painting – mistakenly, of course, because a bee-line in such a place is always a meander. We could not understand how we had by-passed it before. The painting is big, the lady languorous, and the whole thing screams 'Look at me!'.

Nina de Callias was the beautiful, estranged wife of the editor of *Le Figaro*. She was a pianist and poet, and held one of Paris' extravagant salons, frequented by the most talented of Paris society. She died at forty, after a spectacular and strenuous life of sex, alcohol and violent highs and lows. We can't help wondering about this reputation. In Manet's painting of her she has the look of someone exhausted and satisfied after a morning of making biscuits for her women's guild.

The design for the cushion has all the fluidity of a textile, yet with the placed precision of Japanese art; the gold leaf had been suggested with highlights of metallic gold thread and the overall effect is one of great richness. The design is worked simply in tent stitch, and we have outlined the fans in stem stitch for extra definition, though this is quite optional.

## Marking the canvas and following the chart

Cut the canvas to size and bind the edges with masking tape. The design does not have to be marked on the canvas; just follow the color chart on page 57. Remember that the squares represent the canvas intersections, not the holes. Each square represents one tent stitch.

The chart is divided into units of 10 squares by 10 squares to make it easier to follow. Before beginning to stitch, it may be helpful to mark out your canvas in similar units of 10 squares by 10 squares with an HB pencil or permanent marker in a suitable color. Also, we suggest marking the top of the canvas so that, if you turn the canvas while stitching, you will still know where the top is.

## Stitches used

TENT stitch (1), STEM stitch (7). For stitch instructions see page 140.

## Stitching the design

The whole thread of Zephyr wool has been used throughout (4 strands). Five strands of the metallic gold have been used.

Begin in any area you wish. It might be easiest to start at the top right-hand corner, 4–5cm (1½–2in) in from the corner, working horizontally from one block of color to another.

This design can be worked entirely in TENT stitch (1) if you wish, but we have used STEM stitch (7) for the outlining. The outlining has been painted on the chart in a slightly heavier color to show it up against the TENT stitch. See the color chart and the made up cushion for the position. If you find there are spaces once you have worked the STEM stitch (7), 'fill in' with TENT stitch (1) in the relevant colors.

## Making up instructions

When the design has been sewn, the needlepoint may need to be stretched back into shape (see stretching instructions on page 138). Then make it up into a cushion as shown on page 142.

# APPLES AND ORANGES

## BY PAUL CÉZANNE

'Is art not a priesthood which requires pure souls who belong to it entirely?'

In Paris, the first of the Impressionist group that Cézanne met was Pissarro, and through him, the other painters at the Café Guerbois. The role he played in the group was that of *enfant terrible*, sullen and rebellious, although, as Mary Cassatt wrote, 'I found I had misjudged his appearance. Far from being fierce or cut-throat, he had the gentlest nature possible'. Cézanne considered Pissarro his master, and through him learned to stand back and allow nature to speak for herself, relinquishing black and brown and building up his pictures in luminous tones. He felt he 'could paint for a hundred years, a thousand years, without stopping, and I would still feel as though I knew nothing'.

The painting we have adapted for the placemat is one of his most delicious still lifes of fruit, *Apples and Oranges*. He used the same props again and again, arranging his objects with obsessive precision. Every piece was turned and held to create lyricism in the arrangement, with instinctive judgement and speed, probably sending his poor wife Hortense, out to 'get more sprouting onions, long shoots, a bit yellowing, not those glitzy supermarket packs that are only fit for eating!'.

Cézanne's glorious use of pigment makes his fruits earthy and solid. Under his flat brushstrokes, the heart of the object is still sensed, be it skeleton of tree or core of apple. His still lifes are seen from above, letting the maximum image show.

His portraits were also still lifes, the nature of the sitter almost irrelevant. Irritated by one respectfully silent, but wilting, sitter, he asked 'Do apples move?' He was often dissatisfied and frustrated, sometimes ripping canvases in anger, feeling 'like the man with a gold coin, and unable to spend it'.

The landscape needlework shown on page 13 has a marvellous flowing quality, satin stitch follows the movement of the brushstrokes, the tiny tent stitches imitate the water. The number of greens in nature is infinite – she conceals herself so modestly in secret layering, in what Cézanne calls 'a floating smile of sharp intelligence'.

Much has been written about Cézanne's new vision. His dragonfly eye saw nature broken into sharply defined geometric shapes: the cylinder, the sphere and the cone, anticipating the Cubists, illuminating their path. Such painting was not only new to him. It became art's launch pad into the twentieth century.

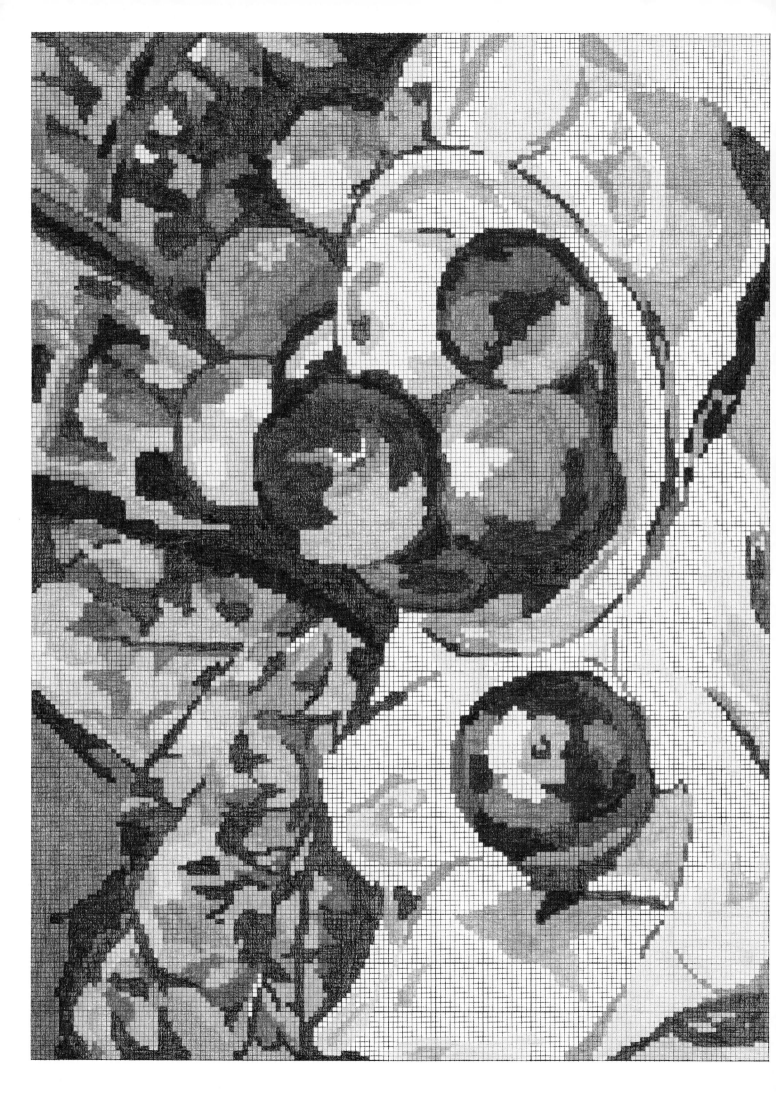

## STITCHING DETAILS

Finished size of design:
37 x 27.5cm (14½ x 11in)

Yarn colors and quantities

| | DMC Laine Zephyr | | Skeins |
|---|---|---|---|
| | 100 | White | 6 |
| | 317 | Charcoal | 6 |
| | 842 | Beige | 3 |
| | 3043 | Heather | 2 |
| | 762 | Gray blue | 3 |
| | 799 | Sky blue | 2 |
| | 524 | Eau de nil green | 3 |
| | 712 | Lemon | 2 |
| | 422 | Yellow ocher | 3 |
| | 977 | Orange | 2 |
| | 358 | Terracotta | 3 |
| | 350 | Flame | 3 |
| | 953 | Dark terracotta | 4 |
| | 300 | Maroon | 3 |

## Canvas

14-gauge white mono de luxe
Size: 47 x 38cm (18½ x 15in)

## Other materials

Tapestry needle, size 20
Ruler or tape measure
Masking tape for binding the canvas
Sharp scissors for cutting the canvas
Embroidery scissors
Sharp HB pencil or fine permanent marker in
suitable color
Eraser

Before beginning to stitch, please read the
general information on page 138.

## Cutting the canvas and following the chart

Cut the canvas to size and bind the edges with masking tape. The design does not have to be marked out on the canvas; just follow the color chart on page 62. Remember that the squares represent the canvas intersections, not the holes. Each square represents one tent stitch.

The chart is divided into units of 10 squares by 10 squares to make it easier to follow. Before beginning to stitch, it may be helpful to mark your canvas in similar units of 10 squares by 10 squares with an HB pencil or permanent marker. Also, we suggest marking the top of the canvas so that, if you turn the canvas while stitching, you will still know where the top is.

## Stitches used

TENT stitch (1) is used throughout. For stitch instructions, see page 140.

## Stitching the design

Use the whole thread of Zephyr wool (4 strands). It might be easiest to start at the top right-hand corner, 4–5cm (1½–2in) in from the corner, working horizontally from one block of color to another.

## Making up instructions

After sewing, the needlepoint may need to stretched back into shape (see page 138). Then make it up into a placemat as shown on page 144. This design would also look wonderful as an opulent cushion or framed as a picture.

# TEXTILES

We used glorious sources for our belts and hats – a zigzag fringed shawl on a Monet portrait, the flounced skirt of a Spanish ballerina, *Lola de Valence* painted by Manet in 1862, and chenille fabric thrown over a table in a Monticelli still life (Cézanne and Van Gogh were both fascinated with his textural experiments, Van Gogh saying, 'I sometimes think I am continuing that man'). All three have stunning colors, and show how the artist broke down the organized patterns into suggestions and iridescent janglings of refracted light.

To translate a fabric into needlepoint, it is not necessary to copy it. A more interesting effect can be achieved by suggesting the design, rather than imitating it. Half-close your eyes so the pattern is not sharp. What stands out? Which flashes of tone jump out at you? Yellow flowers, white outlining – exaggerate those elements. What detail is lost and what dominates? Be an Impressionist – does the fabric shine, does the light graze the velvet, does lurex melt, can you hear the insects buzzing in the flowers? Such paintings are excellent for making us see in sweeps, bold and loose.

In the same way the Impressionist painters were not hidebound by the need for a finished surface, or by one style of brushstroke, we too can absorb the idea of variety, vitality, a carnival of color. The peonies chair on page 107 and the Giverny chair on page 11 had their outlines scribbled on paper and then, without losing their spontaneity, traced quickly through onto the canvas using indelible felt pens, blocking in patches of color, enough indication to follow the picture. It should be excitingly imprecise. It becomes the combination of your imagination and the original piece – there are no boundaries, no-one to say it should, it shouldn't. This is personal interpretation!

The scope to paint beautiful textiles was greater in the Impressionist days than it is today (in other times and other places painters employed specialist velvet painters and specialist lace painters, rather in the way a builder subcontracts to a tiler or electrician). The fabrics were delicious – lace flounces, silk ruffles, hats, striped taffetas, brocades, all worn as a matter of course. Today ingenuity may be required to recreate the ubiquitous denim but it doesn't have the same decorative appeal.

Needlepoint accessories can be very striking, but, because of its inflexible nature, it is best for something that doesn't need movement, like a belt, hat, bag or waistcoat. This belt can be adapted by extending the pattern, just work as much as you need. It isn't difficult to find beautiful old buckles – though do find the buckle before the needlepoint is done, and adapt the width accordingly. A wonderful find, like our emerald and gold enamel clasp, may give you unthought-of ideas for color and design.

## STITCHING DETAILS

Finished size of design:
76 x 6½cm (30 x 2½in)

Yarn colors and quantities

| | DMC Laine Zephyr | | Skeins |
|---|---|---|---|
| | 310 | Black | 7 |
| | 3047 | Butter | 2 |
| | 3078 | Lemon | 3 |
| | 951 | Pale orange | 2 |
| | 977 | Burnt orange | 3 |
| | 301 | Rust | 2 |
| | 350 | Flame | 3 |
| | 640 | Taupe | 2 |
| | 320 | Jade green | 2 |
| | 911 | Emerald | 3 |

### Canvas

14-gauge white mono deluxe
Size: 86 x 17cm (34 x 6½in)

### Other materials

Tapestry needle, size 20
Ruler or tape measure
Masking tape for binding the canvas
Sharp scissors for cutting the canvas
Embroidery scissors
Sharp HB pencil or fine permanent marker in suitable color
Eraser

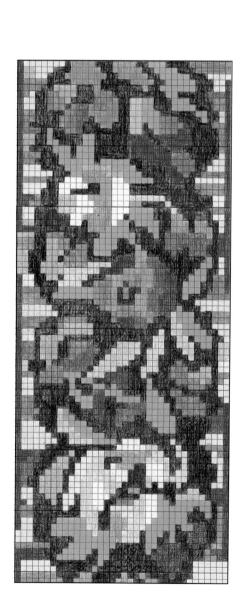

## Marking the canvas and following the chart

Cut the canvas to size and bind the edges with masking tape. The design does not have to be marked out on the canvas; just follow the color chart on the left. Remember that the squares represent the canvas intersections, not the holes. Each square represents one tent stitch.

The chart is divided into units of 10 squares by 10 squares to make it easier to follow. Before beginning to stitch, it may be helpful to mark out your canvas in similar units of 10 squares by 10 squares with an HB pencil or permanent marker in a suitable color. Also, we suggest marking the top of the canvas so that, if you turn the canvas while stitching, you will still know where the top is.

Our belt measures 76cm (30in) in length which, when made up, will fit a

66cm (26in) waist. You will need to repeat the pattern five times. This chart is a 15cm (6in) pattern repeat.

## Stitches used
TENT stitch (1) is used throughout. For stitch instructions see page 140.

## Stitching the design
The whole thread (4 strands) is used throughout.

Begin in any area you wish. It might be easiest to start at the top right-hand corner, 4–5cm (1½–2in) in from the corner, working horizontally from one block of color to another. Repeat the pattern as many times as you need. Remember to make the belt at least 10cm (4in) longer than the measurement of your waist. If you intend using a conventional buckle rather than a clasp, the belt will need to be even longer to allow for the 'flap-over'.

## Making up instructions
When the design has been sewn, the needlepoint may need to be stretched back into shape (see stretching instructions on page 138). Then make it up into a belt as shown. A beautiful antique buckle was found at an antique shop. We couldn't believe our luck – it was perfect with the design. It is made of enamel and looks Spanish.

Another idea would be to use the pattern repeat to make a border around a window, door or skirting board.

# ABSTRACTS

If we take a section of an Impressionist painting, half-close our eyes until the divided tones merge, we can persuade ourselves we are floating in color, and for a moment there is nothing but sunshine and reflections. Step back a pace or two and even the most engulfing swirls take form. These painters were people who understood the sensuality of paint, gift wrapping it, in Renoir's words, in 'pink and golden mists', and spectacular ribbons, and layer upon layer of iridescent tissue, so that we could be enriched.

Look at the beautiful waterlily paintings in the Orangerie in Paris, the extraordinary enveloping canvases that grew out of Impressionism and teeter on abstraction's edge. If we can suspend the mind, and just be swept up in what surrounds us, the impact is piercing, a river of energy, color and shape that exhilarates and enriches, at a level usually untouched . . . we just have to learn the language to tap into the river. How many of us ever give a thought to our souls, placidly slumped, hoping for a little injection of beauty. Here are grasses with waving poppies, here a glorious dimply girl, sea wild, similar skies . . . thank you, murmurs the soul, delicious, yum yum.

By looking at these paintings we can make abstractions by magnifying detail, ignoring context, discarding barriers. Monet was the greatest exponent of trying to see the world through innocent eyes, in pure color and pure shape. The tiny Marmottan Museum houses some of Monet's late work, where, with failing eyesight and laser vision, he pushed Impressionism to the brink of abstraction. If you come straight from the gardens, with a mind saturated with images, it is easy to recognize what you see – and what you see are the last doors of realism beginning to tremble, before being flattened by those who followed.

It is not difficult to adapt a design for needlepoint. Don't be nervous – the only way to begin is bravely, and do what the painters did. Draw what you see. Don't think about the final result, only about the shapes and sensations in front of you. The only rule is to work boldly and trust your instinct!

We used two paintings for our abstract pieces – a Cézanne and a Cassatt. Mary Cassatt painted a portrait of her sister Lydia sitting on a park bench. Her coat is a marvellous mishmash of color and we took a small section of it and began experimenting. The paint was stroked onto the open canvas with similar looseness to Cassatt's, but the transition into yarn gives another dimension – the result is a very dense textile of random shapes and tones. This design would look marvellous on an antique chair, so unexpected.

The Cézanne landscape of Mont Sainte-Victoire fell naturally into its own shapes. It has pleasing simplified blocks because, as we all know, Cézanne painted his geometric slabs with needlepoint in mind.

STITCHING DETAILS

Finished size of design:
37 x 37cm (14½ x 14½in)

Yarn colors and quantities

| DMC Laine Colbert | | | Skeins |
|---|---|---|---|
| | 7713 | Charcoal | 1 |
| | 7226 | Plum | 4 |
| | 7223 | Pale mauve | 6 |
| | 7920 | Flame red | 2 |
| | 7176 | Burnt orange | 4 |
| | 7175 | Orange | 3 |
| | 7173 | Apricot | 5 |
| | 7928 | Pale turquoise | 6 |
| | 7692 | Turquoise | 2 |
| | 7333 | Jade green | 5 |
| | 7472 | Gold | 3 |
| | 7745 | Lemon | 3 |
| | 7506 | Cinnamon | 2 |
| | 7371 | Pale green | 4 |
| | 7512 | Taupe | 3 |

Canvas

12-gauge white mono deluxe
Size: 47 x 47cm (18½ x 18½in)

Other materials

Tapestry needle, size 18 or 20
Ruler or tape measure
Masking tape for binding the canvas
Sharp scissors for cutting the canvas
Embroidery scissors
Sharp HB pencil or fine permanent marker in
suitable color
Eraser

Before beginning to stitch, please read the
general information on page 138.

## Marking the canvas and following the chart

Cut the canvas to size and bind the edges with masking tape. The design does not have to be marked out on the canvas; just follow the color chart on page 71. Remember that the squares represent the canvas intersections, not the holes. Each square represents one TENT stitch.

The chart is divided into units of 10 squares by 10 squares to make it easier to follow. Before beginning to stitch, it may be helpful to mark out your canvas in similar units of 10 squares by 10 squares with an HB pencil or permanent marker in a suitable color. Also, we suggest marking the top of the canvas so that, if you turn the canvas while stitching, you will still know where the top is.

## Stitches used

TENT stitch (1), Reversed TENT stitch (1a) ⊡. For stitch instructions see page 140.

## Stitching the design

The whole thread of tapestry wool is used throughout.

Begin in any area you wish. It might be easiest to start at the top right-hand corner, 4–5cm (1½–2in) in from the corner, working horizontally from one block of color to another.

The symbols on the chart show the areas where reversed TENT stitch (1a) has been used.

## Making up instructions

After sewing, the needlepoint may need to be stretched back into shape (see instructions on page 138). Then make it up into a cushion as shown on page 142.

# STRAWBERRIES
## BY PIERRE-AUGUSTE RENOIR

'You are a friend of Renoir's. You should advise him to give up painting. You can see for yourself he's not very good at it.'

Manet to Monet

Renoir believed there were already enough ugly things in life, and didn't choose to create more by painting them. He wanted his work to be joyful. Today, the language of art is often a regurgitation of anguish and from such a standpoint, it is easy, and wrong, for us to dismiss Renoir as just a chocolate box painter, and not even tastebud-inflaming Belgian chocolates – more like yellow fondant and strawberry creams.

The panels in the cupboard are a 'Michelin Three-Star' dessert: peaches by Cézanne, grapes by Monet, cherries and strawberries by Renoir. We think the whole effect is charming – certainly working little panels like these is very satisfying, and there is a primitive quality to the cupboard that's quite naïve. If you cannot find such a cupboard, nor have an open-to-persuasion carpenter, little pictures like these could be surface mounted and a beading placed around them. To 'age' such a piece of furniture, we can recommend nothing more effective than shunting it back and forth in a van for a year, trying to find the right location to photograph it!

It was a deliberate choice to use Renoir and Monet together. They painted side by side in the early intoxicating days of breaking painting rules. Sometimes it's hard to distinguish their paintings during this period. Like most changes, Impressionism happened naturally, almost imperceptibly, but the main leap seems to have been when the two of them were working so closely and excitingly together at the end of the 1860s.

They had much in common. During financially fraught times both felt themselves to be failures. Many of their self-doubts were shared; both were familiar with the isolated pain of vulnerability. Renoir, however, kept his feelings private and the ease with which he handled himself socially was something that eluded Monet, who was no graduate of Charm School. Renoir's gentle way wooed the haute-bourgeoisie and probably did much to dispel the prejudices against Impressionists.

Renoir was first crippled by lack of money and then by rheumatism. As he grew older, he was unable to move his limbs, and needed two people to carry him. His fingers curved towards the wrists, and his skin was so tender that he could not grip a brush handle without padding his hand with cushions of cloth. When he had finished painting, the brush had to be removed – he couldn't open his fingers himself. His paintings deny this agony – once at the easel, the rainbow brushstrokes palpitated with life and happiness, burning even brighter with the spirit that had ignited his early work.

## STITCHING DETAILS

Finished size of design:
15 x 15cm (6 x 6in)

Yarn colors and quantities

| | DMC Laine Zephyr | | Skeins |
|---|---|---|---|
| | 746 | Cream | 1 |
| | 3078 | Yellow | 1 |
| | 402 | Apricot | 1 |
| | 977 | Orange | 1 |
| | 358 | Terracotta | 1 |
| | 350 | Flamingo | 2 |
| | 953 | Rust | 1 |
| | 408 | Beige | 2 |
| | 406 | Ginger | 1 |
| | 3013 | Lime green | 1 |
| | 522 | Jacobean green | 1 |
| | 319 | Forest green | 1 |
| | 928 | Dull blue | 2 |
| | 929 | Marine blue | 1 |
| | 413 | Charcoal | 1 |

Mixed colors

| | 402/408 |
|---|---|

Canvas

14-gauge white mono deluxe
Size: 25 x 25cm (10 x 10in)

Other materials

Tapestry needle, size 20
Ruler or tape measure
Masking tape for binding the canvas
Sharp scissors for cutting the canvas
Embroidery scissors
Sharp HB pencil or fine permanent marker in
suitable color
Eraser

Before beginning to stitch, please read the
general information on page 138.

---

On hearing of Renoir's death, Monet wrote from Giverny: 'You can't imagine how painful the loss of Renoir has been to me. With him goes part of my own life.'

### Cutting the canvas and following the chart

Cut the canvas to size and bind the edges with masking tape. The design does not have to be marked out on the canvas; just follow the color chart above. Remember that the squares represent the canvas intersections, not the holes. Each square represents one tent stitch.

The chart is divided up into units of 10 squares by 10 squares to make it easier to follow. Before beginning to stitch, it may be helpful to mark out your canvas in similar units of 10 squares by 10 squares with an HB pencil or permanent marker in a suitable color. Also, we suggest marking the top of the canvas so that, if you turn the canvas while stitching, you will still know where the top is.

### Stitches used

TENT stitch (1) and STEM stitch (7). For stitch instructions see page 140.

## Stitching the design

The whole thread of Zephyr wool (4 strands) with the exception of the outlining of the strawberries, the outlining on the bowl and the stems where 2 strands have been used. An explanation on splitting wool is on page 139. The wool has been mixed in certain areas and is indicated on the color key.

Begin with TENT stitch (1) in any area you wish. It might be easiest to start at the top right-hand corner 4–5cm (1½–2in) in from the corner, working horizontally from one block of color to another. We have used STEM stitch (7) to outline the strawberries, the bowl and the stems. Refer to the photograph of the stitched panel for the position. The STEM stitch (7) can be put on afterwards.

## Making up instructions

When the design has been sewn, the needlepoint may need to be stretched back into shape (see stretching instructions on page 138). We have sewn four separate designs and made them into panels for a cupboard. If you prefer, you can frame the Strawberries or make it into a cushion – see page 142.

# GARDENS

'I am good for nothing except painting and gardening.'

Claude Monet

Giverny – not a garden, but *the* garden. The place Monet created with such simple instructions as:

Sowing: around 300 pots poppies, 60 sweet peas, around 60 pots white Agrimony – 30 yellow Agrimony – Blue sage – Blue waterlilies in beds (greenhouse). From 15th–25th lay the dahlias down to root, plant out those with shoots before I get back. Don't forget the lily bulbs. Should the Japanese peonies arrive, plant them immediately if weather permits, taking care initially to protect buds from the cold, as much as from the heat of the sun. Get down to pruning: plant out the little nasturtiums, keep a close eye on the gloxinia, orchids, etc in the greenhouse as well as the plants under frames. Trim the borders as arranged, put wires in for the clematis and climbing roses as soon as Picard has done the necessary. Plant cuttings from the rose trees at the pond around manure in the hen huts. . .

The gardens have been breathtakingly and faithfully restored. And of course, because Giverny is magic, and because this is a story, it is the place for solitude, to be alone and far from alone. It is a garden where the pathway stones crunch, not only with our feet but with remembered easels' indentations, and ghosts smile, amused, astonished. Do you see the lines, Claude, with their maps and Minoltas, do you hover in this incandescent air, are your hands forever on the balustrade of the terrace?

We eat baguettes on the verandah, spreading ourselves among the cameras and reflectors, the lifelines of photography, sitting in the shadows of the masters. There are some local painters in the garden and every so often the smell of oil paints wafts in the air – real smells, or part of the collective unconscious of the place? The day is unusually hot for spring, the bread is dry, and we crave melon and ginger, a chilled Sancerre, sardines grilled with herbs, an idle afternoon. We should sit by the pond, parasols gently rotating, sensing conversations overheard in the weighted air. In this shimmering place the mind leapfrogs between past and present, and through half-closed eyes is it not possible to make out Renoir and Pissarro, Degas and Cassatt?

Giverny is at its most outrageously theatrical in spring. Irises, all lapping tongues and pie-frill edges, brown, yellow, purple, dark plum, almost black, surely this is crimped silk on wire stems, pleated Fortuny fabric? Oriental poppies, massive blooms compressed like folded parachutes, needing only the tiniest slit in their buds to start the explosion. Tulips levitate among forget-me-nots – we collect the fallen blooms and thread them through a buttonhole against our overwhelmed hearts.

Chestnut blossoms in our hair, azaleas on the inner eye. An afternoon heat haze hangs over the water gardens, August sultriness in May. Children

*Miniature picture adapted from* The Artist's Garden at Giverny *which Monet painted in 1895, showing the stunning variety of peonies that he planted.*

*Previous page: Giverny and the overflowing world of the waterlilies. The needlepoint on the chairs was inspired by Monet's prolific paintings of this once-seen-never-forgotten water garden.*

sit on the Japanese bridge and paint the trees viridian and the pond ultramarine, when it is clearly charcoal and aubergine. What are they seeing? How do we condition the young to believe water always to be blue? One boy daubs many colors in different directions, really seeing what he is looking at. There is hope.

The bridge is painted in what we call Giverny Green – it seems a strange choice for Monet to have made, among the thousand greens in the garden this is sympathetic to none. Its artificiality jars and yet it is now so much part of terrace, trellis and wisteria bridge that we can't imagine an alternative. At the Old Mill House in London, we rebuilt a ruined outhouse and on concealed timbers found the original color to be Almost-Giverny Green. Perhaps it lacked the hint of emerald, but it was close, so we used it to paint the new walls. It looked awful. The local Preservation Society protested, so did our neighbors. We said 'But this was the original color and besides, it looks stunning at Giverny.' We repainted it cream and grew wisteria up it. There's a lesson here somewhere.

Three women are having a conversation near the bench where Monet always sat, cigarette dangling. They discuss how he could have painted the same scene day after day, year after year. And why. Why? Can they not imagine an obsession as slippery as water grass, with every change of light becoming a new elusive variation? Have they never listened to the same piece of music twice, twenty times? Or thought: this is great sex, what nuances will I find next time, will I appreciate more, will it be different, let's have a bit more of this here, a bit more of that there! Let's do it again because it's compulsive!

We try to see what Monet and the other paint gurus saw, as we translate their images into yarn and canvas, sometimes acknowledging brushstrokes, sometimes pinpricks of dazzling light, always a mouthwatering celebration of nature. In the heat there are accompaniments that go with the paintings – a symphony of crickets and bees, a sky bleached pale, buttercups with varnished faces neon in the sun.

The hotel in Giverny, a few yards (as the blossom flies) from Monet's house, has wallpaper with waterlilies slanted into the eaves. The river is across the road, the poplars like guardians of the dusk. There is the story that as soon as the locals at Epte saw Monet become attached to some poplars, they marked them to be cut down. He had to pay to delay this until he had finished the series of paintings he was doing. We look at trees and hills with unveiled eyes, because of what a handful of artists showed us, ensuring that the way we see nature will never be the same again.

We are intoxicated by Giverny and the hotel's position is spectacular. Even a chef who appears to work in an abattoir, and bedroom walls made from cardboard, cannot spoil the mood. The man in the next room sings

*This picture says it all: lunch is over, the summer light dapples, you can almost hear the cuckoos. Monet painted this at Giverny in 1873 – the atmosphere he created is almost tangible today.*

*Strangers in the Night* in Spanish, and then the Hallelujah Chorus. The owls call, and in the morning there are cockerels and wood pigeons and cuckoos. The air smells of apples and the expectation of summer.

On days when the garden is closed, people stand on their car roofs trying to see over the wall, like hungry children outside a baker's window drooling over the goodies. When Monet created the garden the wall was generously low, and an unsuspecting driver on the road to Vernon could suddenly be assaulted with rainbows. Flowers are planted as close as they can be without choking each other, the effect is exuberant chaos, but it has been achieved like a military maneuver. Flowers, borders, bushes, hedges change all the time, colors resonate, combinations replacing each other in waves – great festooning arbors, overhead hoops trailing roses and the ground nasturtium-carpeted. In dazzling tunnels of nodding blooms, we become skipping flower fairies, overwhelmed by the explosions of opulence. Monet may have been mocking and austere in Paris, but here he was truly serene, forgetting the rest of civilization in single-minded dedication.

More and more of his contemporaries came to Giverny. He'd send a car to meet them, so they couldn't be late, nor outstay their welcome. Nothing was permitted to interrupt his routine. They came to witness the phenomena of his garden while outsiders had to look over the wall or through the gate. Into which group do we fall now? It seems more the second than the first – we can walk through the gate but the barrier of time keeps us a few steps removed. It is only in certain silences that the dividing years can begin to approach each other.

For over forty years Monet painted at Giverny. When he finally died at 86, he wanted his funeral to be private, and there were fewer than a dozen people there on that foggy morning. A book of Baudelaire's poems lay open in his studio on a page that read 'What do you love, extraordinary stranger? I love the clouds. . . the clouds that pass. . . up there. . . the wonderful clouds!'

The coffin was draped in black. His last remaining friend, Clemenceau, tore down a faded cretonne curtain printed with blue hydrangeas, forget-me-nots, periwinkles, and replaced the black shroud with all the colors of the skies Monet so loved. It was thus that Claude Monet, who understood the changes of nature so well, was buried in Giverny's little cemetery.

*A Victorian shawl, which we embroidered with the tulips Monet loved to grow, photographed in his famous boat.*

# WISTERIA

## FROM MONET'S GIVERNY

Wisteria isn't an image we usually associate with Monet, but for those visiting Giverny in late May it is something unlikely to be forgotten. The flowers hang from the bridge, mauve and white like pendulous breasts drawn by the pond below. Soon they must touch the water, perhaps next year, always next year. You feel they should smell overpoweringly, but their scent is subtle and the blasts of fragrance are from the azaleas growing close by, not from these heavenly dangling blooms on their knuckled branches.

In Monet's day the mauve wisteria grew at the top, the white at the bottom. Now the mauve looks out onto the main pond and the white faces the pool where the boat lays, where the willows decay, where the debris gathers after a storm. To us, they are the most overtly ostentatious, attention-demanding display that spring offers. Who can walk past without touching?

Monet painted them when his eyesight was deteriorating but was afraid that an operation would leave him blind. His vision made the wisteria chaotic, you feel the frustration of his brush, the speed. A branch is thrown across the canvas, leaves and petals loaded onto it, scrawls of emerald, viridian, gold, touches of precise pink, on an impossible hyacinth sky.

In the late afternoon when the sun falls behind the poplars, these flowers that seem to be illuminated internally have their wattage dimmed. We sit at the place where Monet painted, a point where the yellow water irises grow, half-turned away from the Folies Bergères spectacle of the wisteria bridge, and wonder why he didn't paint them more. Perhaps spring is too short to do everything . . . a season of such riches in a concertina of weeks, with every direction demanding attention.

Our rug shows blooms and branches, the colors are dull pinks, grays and faded mauves, on a background of soft gray-green. The leaves are tipped with sunshine, the branches weave through the trellis, there is a suggestion of Japanese bridge. The rug is worked in tent stitch on large hole canvas using tapestry wool double – it grows deceptively quickly, particularly if you persuade someone else to start at the other end.

One of our Glorafilia girls fell on the rug with great excitement – her bedroom is stencilled and festooned with wisteria motifs and she lusted after two such rugs, one for either side of the bed. Not a weekend's project, we said. Using the same chart on smaller gauges of canvas you could make a stool top, oblong cushion or, if such is your wont and eyesight, even a matchbox cover. Alternatively, do as we did – hang it from a bridge in the garden.

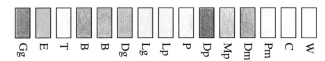

STITCHING DETAILS

Finished size of design:
92 x 135 cm (36 x 53in)

Yarn colors and quantities

| Colors | | DMC Laine Colbert Skeins | | Appletons Hanks | |
|---|---|---|---|---|---|
| | White | Blanc | 16 | 991 | 2½ |
| | Custard | 7579 | 16 | 841 | 2½ |
| | Pale mauve | 7260 | 20 | 884 | 3 |
| | Dark mauve | 7262 | 17 | 602 | 2½ |
| | Mid-pink | 7223 | 9 | 142 | 1½ |
| | Dark-pink | 7226 | 4 | 143 | ½ |
| | Peach | 7191 | 5 | 877 | ¼ |
| | Light-pink | 7213 | 5 | 711 | ¼ |
| | Light grass | 7361 | 45 | 251A | 7 |
| | Dark grass | 7384 | 40 | 402 | 6 |
| | Beige | 7521 | 16 | 182 | 2½ |
| | Brown | 7465 | 14 | 301 | 2 |
| | Turquoise | 7323 | 43 | 522 | 6½ |
| | Emerald | 7542 | 36 | 831 | 5½ |
| | Gray-green | 7337 | 220 | 966 | 33 |

Canvas

7-gauge cream rug canvas interlocked
Size: 102 x 145cm (40 x 57in)

Other materials

Tapestry needle, size 16
Ruler or tape measure
Masking tape for binding the canvas
Sharp scissors for cutting the canvas
Embroidery scissors
Sharp HB pencil or fine permanent marker in
suitable color
Eraser

Before beginning to stitch, please read the
general information on page 138.

## Marking the canvas and following the chart

Cut the canvas to size and bind the edges with tape. The design does not have
to be marked on the canvas; just follow the chart. The squares represent the
canvas intersections, not the holes. Each square represents one TENT stitch.

The chart is divided into units of 10 squares by 10 squares to make it
easier to follow. Before stitching, it may help to mark your canvas in similar
units with an HB pencil or permanent marker. Mark the top of the canvas so
that, if you turn the canvas while stitching, you know where the top is.

## Stitches used

TENT stitch (1) has been used throughout. See instructions on page 140.

## Stitching the design

The thread has been used double. Thread 2 threads of the same color into
the needle at the same time. It may be easiest to start at the top right-hand
corner 4–5cm (1½–2in) in from the corner, working horizontally in blocks
of color. If you do not have a frame to fit the rug, place the rug on a table and
put weights on top to stop it moving; sit at the table and begin stitching,
moving the position of the rug as necessary.

## Making up instructions

After sewing, the rug will need to be stretched back into shape (see page
138). Then make it up into a rug as shown on page 144.

# THE CUP OF TEA

## BY MARY CASSATT

'Degas persuaded me to send no more to the Salon and to exhibit with his friends in the group of Impressionists. I accepted with joy. At last I could work with complete independence without concerning myself with the eventual judgement of a jury. I already knew who were my true masters. I admired Manet, Courbet and Degas. I hated conventional art. I began to live.'

*The Cup of Tea* was chosen for its serenity, a charming moment captured, and interpreted into needlepoint with perfect simplicity, tiny flat stitches in wool, cotton and metal thread. We arrange table, lace and china around the picture, and wonder how often Mary Cassatt stood exactly where we are now, on the verandah at Giverny. Did that Pennsylvanian primness succumb to pressing a fallen blossom in her notebook? Did the unsentimental eye gather in the glorious garden? And does it still?

When the painting was shown in 1881, the critic J.K. Huysmans called it 'tender, contemplative, a fine sense of Parisian elegance. And it is a special indication of her talent that Miss Cassatt, who I believe is American, paints French women for us'. And what women! Her portraits, particularly of the mother and child relationship, show gentle, powerful insight.

They are simple studies, no frills or pretentions – the mother is sometimes preoccupied, the child open and direct. Hands reassure, comfort, enclose, so brilliantly that we can feel the child slipping off the lap, wriggling, balancing itself, exploring the mother with familiar caresses. These paintings are all the more poignant as she was childless.

In 1866, when she was 22, Cassatt came to Europe to study art. On her decision to become an artist, her banker father, supportive and encouraging, said 'I'd rather see her dead!' While he eventually mellowed, she remained a curiosity to her family, who humored what they saw as eccentricity. Years later, after establishing herself alongside the Impressionists, she again crossed the Atlantic and the Philadelphia Ledger wrote: 'Mary Cassatt, sister of Mr Cassatt, president of the Pennsylvania railroad, returned from Europe yesterday. She has been studying painting in France and owns the smallest Pekinese dog in the world'. We shall never know her comments, but as she was known for being opinionated, let's assume it was worthy of her reputation. An interesting lady, she would have been as much at home in this century as her own.

In the group, she was closest to Degas. The friendship was based on mutual uncompromising devotion to art. He became her mentor, and she forced him to change his prejudices about women – 'I am not willing to admit that a woman can draw that well', he said, but conceded 'What drawing! What style!'. It was assumed they were lovers. After a typically

STITCHING DETAILS

Finished size of design:
18 x 25.5 cm (7 x 10in)

Yarn colors and quantities
DMC Mouliné Spécial

| | | | Skeins |
|---|---|---|---|
| | Blanc | White | 2 |
| | 963 | Sugar pink | 3 |
| | 739 | Cream | 1 |
| | 3733 | Rose pink | 2 |
| | 3731 | Dark rose pink | 2 |
| | 950 | Peach | 1 |
| | 407 | Bois de rose | 1 |
| | 3747 | Light blue | 1 |
| | 809 | Sky blue | 2 |

Mixed colors

| | | |
|---|---|---|
| • | 950/407 | |

DMC Broder Medicis

| | | | Skeins |
|---|---|---|---|
| | 8421 | Sap green | 2 |
| | 8426 | Almond green | 1 |
| | 8407 | Jade | 2 |
| | 8414 | Forest green | 1 |
| | 8109 | Pale sienna | 1 |
| | 8105 | Mid-sienna | 2 |
| | 8427 | Eau de nil green | 2 |
| | 8500 | Dark brown | 5 |

Mixed colors

| | | |
|---|---|---|
| • | 8407/8500 | |

| | | |
|---|---|---|
| | DMC Fil or clair (gold thread) (Only a 46cm (18in) length is needed) | 1 spool |

Canvas

18-gauge white mono deluxe
Size: 28 x 35.5cm (11 x 14in)

Other materials

Tapestry needle, size 22
Ruler or tape measure
Masking tape for binding the canvas
Sharp scissors for cutting the canvas
Embroidery scissors
Sharp HB pencil or fine permanent marker in
suitable color
Eraser

Before beginning to stitch, please read the
general information on page 138.

acidic remark of his, she refused to speak to him for several years, so perhaps they were. His remark that she painted a picture as a milliner would make a hat was intended to be complimentary.

On the title page of this book is a painting of Cassatt's sister Lydia, working at a tapestry frame. She sat many times, sewing, crocheting, reading – gentle pursuits, beautifully captured moments – no fish-gutting, or drain-unblocking, thank you. Appropriately, and sadly, this painting is considered the best of them all; shortly after it was completed, Lydia died (this had been a long illness and no direct reflection on needlepoint).

Cassatt, like Monet, tragically suffered from cataracts and we can only guess at the riches lost because of it. She spent the last years of her life blind and alone, though the spirit didn't diminish and visitors were still swept along by blazes of fire and enthusiasm from this formidable old lady. Seeing the mass of scattered flowers at her funeral, one friend fancied he saw her running to fetch canvas and brushes . . . rather as we imagined we saw her this morning, over there, near the peonies, in her white serge jacket.

## Marking the canvas and following the chart

Cut the canvas to size and bind the edges with masking tape. The design does not have to be marked out on the canvas; just follow the color chart on page 91. Remember that the squares represent the canvas intersections, not the holes. Each square represents one TENT stitch.

The chart is divided into units of 10 squares by 10 squares to make it easier to follow. Before beginning to stitch, it may be helpful to mark out your canvas in similar units of 10 squares by 10 squares with an HB pencil or permanent marker in a suitable color. Also, we suggest marking the top of the canvas so that, if you turn the canvas while stitching, you will still know where the top is.

## Stitches used

TENT stitch (1), Reversed TENT stitch (1a) ◣, STEM stitch (7). For stitch instructions see page 140.

## Stitching the design

Two threads of Medicis wool have been used throughout with the exception of the wallpaper and the dark brown outline on the cup where one thread has been used. The whole thread (6 strands) of Coton Mouliné Spécial has been used with the exception of the outline on her nose when one strand has been used. The metallic gold on the cup is used double. The yarn has been mixed in certain areas and this is indicated on the color chart. When the Medicis wool is mixed, use one thread of each color. When Coton Mouliné is mixed, use 3 strands of each color (6 strands equals one thread).

It might be easiest to start at the top right-hand corner 4–5cm (1½–2in) in from the corner, working horizontally from one block of color to another. This design can be worked entirely in TENT stitch if you wish, but if you require a more realistic look, work her left hand in reversed TENT stitch (1a) – this is indicated on the chart. Work the STEM stitch (7) around the cup and saucer in dark brown 8500 and in gold where indicated and outline the nose in flesh 950. If you find there are spaces once you have worked the STEM stitch, 'fill in' with TENT stitches in the relevant colors.

## Making up

Many needlepointers feel experienced enough to stretch and make up their needlework designs into cushions but we always feel that a needlepoint picture should be framed by a professional, who has experience in stretching and framing needlepoint.

# IRISES

## BY VINCENT VAN GOGH

'A painter paints not only with color but also with abnegation and self-denial and a broken heart . . . a horse who is dragging a cab of people who are off to sample the joys of spring.'

In the same way that certain actors can sit silently on a stage and still shout, so some paintings have a presence that is not contained by the limits of the canvas. A Pissarro could hang on a central wall and still look discreet, while a Van Gogh cramped in a corner, would shriek. It's as if the passion applied with the pigment still vibrates there.

Some years ago, in a steaming August Manhattan, unexpectedly seeing a familiar Van Gogh amongst construction work at the Museum of Modern Art was like finding a friend's face in the Kalahari. The painting was *The Starry Night*, the feverish brushstrokes of the paint so strong, its swirls so hypnotic, that without realizing it, the respectful distance between face and paint got smaller and smaller. The attendant said, in Brooklynese, apparently à propos nothing:

'There's a lot of unemployment in New York.'

'What?'

'There's a lot of unemployment in New York.'

'Oh. Really.'

'Your nose touches the painting, lady, I lose my job, and there's a lot of unemployment in New York.'

Van Gogh painted *The Starry Night* at St Remy, the asylum where he finally killed himself. Poor, tormented Vincent. The first painting he did when he arrived there was the *Irises*, which we have used as our project because . . . well, how could we not? It is the most irisy, over-the-top, exuberant, extravagant iris picture of them all. Irises at their zenith of irisness. We have taken a section, doffed our caps in apology as we shuffled the flowers a little, used the mauvest mauves, the most faithful greens, stitched in Van Gogh stitches, shuddering stabs, angular satin. These flowers, more like orchids than irises, more like animals than orchids, with their tongues and grooves and fronds and unlikely folds opening flagrantly to the sun, have been painted by others, then and since, but not like this. This is not just paint flung with wild energy, every stroke is relevant, and even a Redoute exactness couldn't do it better. If only one iris reference goes into the Time Capsule, it should be this.

Van Gogh is usually included with the Impressionists because of their influence on his work, but this is our obsession with titles, names and labels. He is really on his own. He came to Paris in 1886 – the year of the last Impressionist exhibition. Their work must have dazzled him – he was advised by Pissarro to lift the somber shades of his palette, he met Sisley, Monet and Degas, and his work changed drastically to absorb their influences of light and color. Paris overstimulated him, although it did bring a balance and gentleness to his work, but after two years the need for the sun forced him to go south, feeling 'that the colors of the prism are veiled in the mists of the north'.

He had become a virtuoso with his brush, free and loose, dappling and scattering color, but from the time he travelled to the Midi, stress made the same techniques distorted – the paintings are turbulent and wildly emotional. His temperament couldn't support the intensity of an unremitting sun and the disturbing mistral winds.

For the final ten years of his life Vincent was supported by his brother, Theo. Their relationship was extraordinary, left to us in the form of letters to Theo that in these days of telephones would probably not happen. They were locked in a commitment to Vincent's art and the reassurance he needed that Theo believed all the money being spent was worthwhile. The letters let us hear the voice of an articulate and sensitive man – anything but Vincent the Deranged, the myth reinforced by the swirling brushstrokes, tormented olive trees, wild skies. His mental illness debilitated him, but he was actually only ill for spasmodic periods during his last two years. He died at thirty-seven, and Theo died six months later. We can only hope that in 1987 they were both leaning over the shoulder of the auctioneer at Sotheby's, stuffing handkerchiefs in their mouths, when the hammer came down on the *Irises* at $53,900,000.

The painting hangs in the Getty Museum in Malibu, a stretch of coast where sea and rocks are as untamed as anything Vincent painted. No mistral blows. He would have liked it.

### Marking the canvas

Cut the canvas to size and bind the edges with masking tape. This is a combined chart and artwork design. Trace the outline (from pages 152–3) on to the canvas with a permanent marker in a suitable color, using the straight outline as a guide for the edge of the design. Follow the curved lines freely, ignoring the canvas grid. Trace the straight edge. When tracing straight lines use your discretion and mark the outline on the closest thread of the canvas.

If you are experienced it is not necessary to trace the fine red lines, which are a guide to show where the colors change. These red lines can be disregarded or can be put on afterwards, freehand, in a different color. A beginner may find it easier to follow the design by tracing the fine lines – do this with a permanent marker in a different color, after you have finished tracing the thick lines.

## STITCHING DETAILS

We suggest only experienced stitchers attempt this project. It is not for beginners.

Finished size of design:
28.5 x 39.5 cm (11¼ x 15½in)

Yarn colors and quantities

| DMC Coton Mouliné Spécial | | | Skeins |
|---|---|---|---|
| | Blanc | White | 2 |
| | 211 | Pale mauve | 3 |
| | 340 | Mid-mauve | 7 |
| | 333 | Dark mauve | 8 |
| | 977 | Orange | 2 |
| | 921 | Burnt orange | 2 |
| | 945 | Apricot | 2 |
| | 3047 | Sand | 3 |
| | 3053 | Taupe | 3 |
| | 3752 | Pale blue | 4 |
| | 954 | Peppermint | 4 |
| | 597 | Turquoise | 5 |
| | 704 | Lime | 4 |
| | 702 | Emerald | 5 |
| | 310 | Black | 9 |

### Canvas

14-gauge white interlock
Size: 38 x 51cm (15 x 20in)

### Other materials

Tapestry needle, size 20
Ruler or tape measure
Masking tape for binding the canvas
Sharp scissors for cutting the canvas
Embroidery scissors
Sharp HB pencil or fine permanent marker in suitable color
Eraser

Before beginning to stitch, please read the general information on page 138.

## Stitches used
TENT stitch (1), SATIN stitch (2), LONG and SHORT stitch (3), STEM stitch (7).

## Stitching the design
The whole thread (6 strands) of Coton Mouliné has been used throughout the picture.

## Stitching the flowers
The instructions on page 140 will show you how to do the stitches. The numbers on the colored artwork refer to the stitch numbers. Look at the photograph of the made-up picture and the colored artwork to show you which color goes where (the arrows show the direction of the stitches). Remember, this is a guide, do not be restricted by it and feel free to experiment.

Stitch the outlines first in STEM stitch (7). Sometimes several rows of STEM stitch (7) are required when the outline is thick, for example, the first iris on the left hand side. All the leaves and flowers are outlined in STEM stitch (7), then 'filled in' with LONG and SHORT stitch (3) in a fairly crude way to imitate brush strokes – follow the arrows for the direction of the stitches. The stems are also outlined in STEM stitch (7) with SATIN stitch (2) inside.

### Following the chart

When you have completed stitching the flowers, follow the color chart behind the irises and 'fill in' the background. Remember that the squares represent the canvas intersections, not the holes. Each square represents one TENT stitch.

The chart is divided into 10 squares by 10 squares to make it easier to follow. Before beginning to stitch the background, it may be helpful to mark out your canvas in similar units of 10 squares by 10 squares with an HB pencil or permanent marker in a suitable color.

### Stitching the background

The background is worked entirely in TENT stitch (1). Begin in any area you wish. It might be easiest to start by 'filling in' the stitches on the edge of the irises at the top left-hand corner of the design and working around the irises. Do not be concerned if you have to compensate by leaving out some stitches as everyone will trace and stitch the outline of the irises in a slightly different way.

### Finishing and making up

Many needlepointers feel experienced enough to stretch and make up their needlework designs into cushions, but we always feel that a needlepoint picture should be framed by a professional, who has experience at stretching and framing needlepoint.

# WATERLILY POND

## BY CLAUDE MONET

'I would like to paint the way a bird sings.'

By the 1880s Monet was earning enough from his paintings to begin serious work on the gardens at Giverny and to create the waterlily pond by diverting a tributary of the River Epte. He planted every known variety of waterlily. In the summer months, framed by aspen and willow and with a floating rainbow of lilies, the pond is magical.

There is something extraordinary about the waterlilies and their microcosmic world. Rooted in earth, sustained by water, everyday emerging into air, opening to the sun. A morning birthing perfectly attuned to the rhythm of the elements. For most of us, it is privilege enough to witness this. In Monet's case he was able to express what he sensed in unerring strokes of his brush.

Monet painted the bridge often in the early waterlily years, before he lowered his focus onto the water alone. To understand his vision perhaps we should look with the heart, not just with the mind. The mind perceives waterlilies, an inverted sky and willows, infused and confused with patterning of grasses beneath the water. Are shadows really shadows or reflections? There is continuous change, the petals open and close in response to the changing light, almost as one watches. Put aside the retina of intellect and what do you see then? The elements merge, nature shows us her most spectacular self, and the magic-lantern is showered with fireworks. As Monet said, 'Give me your hand – let us help one another to observe ever better.'

The master was ageing and could not tolerate disturbance. Alone in the gardens, as he was, the tissue of time prevents our hearing his boots on the wooden bridge, but we too hate the idea of intruders.

Monet painted the bridge in all lights, pink and orchid and autumnal, and most memorably blue in the morning and evening coolness – thousands of suggestions and nuances and persuasive flashes of paint, like fluttering butterfly kisses. It is one of the most frequently reproduced images for cards, posters and books, and actually being in the familiar gardens feels like Alice stepping through the Looking Glass.

The bridge was an irresistible subject for needlepoint. Tiny stitches on canvas can look like thousands of flicks of color. The willows dictated that they be worked in chain stitch because it drops downwards so perfectly, the reeds dictated long and short stitch to look feathery. Each stitch built the color into shapes, and the finished result is a satisfying mosaic that needed much witty weaving in and out of the yarn on the back to counteract needlepointer's crow's-nest syndrome!

*Giverny's Japanese bridge, which seems to float above the waterlily pond, was painted by Monet many times around 1900, and in many variations of light and color.*

# WATERLILIES

## BY CLAUDE MONET

'I have once more taken up things that can't be done: water with grasses weaving on the bottom . . . it's wonderful to see, but it's maddening to try to paint it. These landscapes of water and reflections have become an obsession.'

For the waterlily cushion we worked from nature, but borrowed the background from Monet – the mauve reflections, dark grasses beneath the surface, a breeze wrinkling the limpid pond into moiré. There are just four stitches, tent for the background, brick to suggest the flatness of the lily pads, long and short to make the lily petals curve, stem stitch for emphasis. The flowers are highlighted in cotton to stand out from the leaves. In reality they are like cupped hands, like fat waxed artificial blooms.

Monet's pinnacles and pits continued. His fought-for commercial success and growing international reputation were counteracted by tragedy – he was devastated by the deaths of those closest to him. His eyesight was deteriorating. His friend Clemenceau urged him to continue working, pushing out boundaries, and Monet conceived the *Décorations des Nympheas*, his master work of the water gardens, and a culmination of the years of Giverny paintings.

While painting the panels his eyesight became even worse. After a life of vision, came the fear of days being short, the laser blurring, dear God, please another day, before the candle dims and the grayness blocks the senses. Gates close one by one and the daylight slips. By some sixth sense, and seventh and eighth, he completed the panels. Perhaps light waves became sound waves, perhaps his guardian angels stood to attention (instead of playing hopscotch as usual). His instinct for color and tone allowed him to paint on inspired automatic pilot. He had such a huge fear of failure and suffered terrible rages of despair over work that fell short of his intentions, and with this last work he knew he could not fail. And he did not. He unlocked the chest containing the secrets of light, and claimed them as his own.

The series now hangs in the Orangerie, which is, quite simply, a shrine. Perhaps there should be added to the rules of 'No Smoking, No Spitting', 'No Speaking, No Sudden Movements.' Applause should be allowed, though. It is a surprise to be reminded that these works are something material, called paint on canvas. See them, and light a million metaphoric candles to him.

The chairs on pages 76–7 were inspired by one of Monet's waterlily paintings, brilliant flashes of cerise and emerald, the forerunner of abstraction. Our photograph was taken in the early morning, after a party –

Violet de Brecourt and her lover Lucien had sat by the water until dawn, trying to resolve their crisis. A terrible scene took place, and much weeping. We know the situation was unresolvable – he was, after all, young enough to be her son, and the evidence of her abandoned shoes and poor Lucien's jacket seems horribly clear, but unthinkable.

## Marking the canvas

Cut the canvas to size and bind the edges with masking tape. This is a combined chart and artwork design. Trace the outline (from pages 150–1) on to the canvas with a permanent marker, using the straight outline as a guide for the edge of the design. Follow the curved lines freely, ignoring the canvas grid. Trace the straight edge. When tracing straight lines use your discretion and mark the outline on the closest thread of the canvas.

If you are experienced it is not necessary to trace the red lines, which show where the colors change. These red lines can be disregarded or can be put on afterwards, freehand, in a different color. A beginner may find it easier to follow the design by tracing the fine lines – do this with a permanent marker in a different color, after tracing the thick lines.

## Stitches used

TENT stitch (1), LONG and SHORT stitch (3), BRICK stitch over two threads (4), STEM stitch (7). See page 140 for stitch instructions.

## Stitching the lilies

The whole thread of Zephyr wool (4 strands) and the whole thread of Coton Mouliné Spécial (6 strands) have been used throughout the design. The cream wool 746 has been worked on the leaves. The cream cotton 712 has been worked on the flowers. The color key is the same for both.

The numbers on the colored artwork refer to the stitch numbers. Look at the photograph of the made up cushion and the colored artwork to show you which color goes where. The arrows show the direction of the stitches. Remember, this is a guide, feel free to experiment.

Work the lilies in LONG and SHORT stitch (3) with some edging in STEM stitch (7). The leaves are horizontal BRICK stitch (4) over two threads.

## Following the chart

When you have completed the waterlilies, follow the color chart and 'fill in' the background. Remember that the squares represent the canvas intersections, not the holes. Each square represents one TENT stitch. The chart is divided into units of 10 squares by 10 squares to make it easier to follow. Before stitching the background, it may be helpful to mark your canvas in similar units with an HB pencil or permanent marker.

STITCHING DETAILS

Finished size of design:
33 x 33cm (13 x 13in)

Yarn colors and quantities

| | DMC Laine Zephyr | | Skeins |
|---|---|---|---|
| | 818 | Sugar pink | 2 |
| | 755 | Mid rose pink | 2 |
| | 756 | Dark rose pink | 2 |
| | 523 | Pale sage green | 2 |
| | 522 | Dark sage green | 3 |
| | 989 | Grass green | 3 |
| | 3364 | Apple green | 3 |
| | 3345 | Dark green | 6 |
| | 565 | Bottle green | 5 |
| | 369 | Almond green | 2 |
| | 746 | Cream | 1 |

| | DMC Coton Mouliné Spécial | | Skeins |
|---|---|---|---|
| | 712 | Cream | 1 |
| | 945 | Peach | 2 |
| | 315 | Maroon | 3 |
| | 3042 | Pale mauve | 2 |
| | 3041 | Dark mauve | 2 |

Canvas

12-gauge white interlock
Size: 43 x 43cm (17 x 17in)

Other materials

Tapestry needle, size18 or 20
Ruler or tape measure
Masking tape for binding the canvas
Sharp scissors for cutting the canvas
Embroidery scissors
Sharp HB pencil or fine permanent marker in suitable color
Eraser

Before beginning to stitch, please read the general information on page 138.

## Stitching the background

The background is worked entirely in TENT stitch (1). It might be easiest to start by 'filling in' the stitches on either side of the lilies and working upwards. Do not be concerned if you have to leave out some stitches, as everyone will trace and stitch the outline of the waterlilies in a different way.

## Making up

After sewing, the needlepoint may need to be stretched back into shape (see page 138). Then make it up into a cushion as shown on pages 142–4.

# PEONIES

## BY EDOUARD MANET

*'Our eyes are meet to see with'*

Manet to Proust

Peonies in crimson and cream and the color of guavas, too heavy for their stems, bursting and bruising if touched by disbelieving fingers. We cradle their weight, how very Manet, we say, how very beautiful. Spring overflows ostentatiously onto the pathway . . . tread gently ladies, lest the hems of your skirts disturb the petals as they did a hundred years ago.

What Manet saw, the vision that he committed onto canvas via eye, spirit and hand, was not of the peonies we know, but a dazzling luminous expression, a champagne glass raised to nature, the essence of the flower. He simplified, he edited, he emphasized. He caught the moment the flame was at its most brilliant before it fades, when the energy can no longer be sustained and the petals will drop. Peonies can never be the same again.

Peonies were Manet's favorite flower, he painted them over and over again. We sketched the needlepoint canvas for the chair and then collected the yarns, perhaps thirty shades of crewel wool, then found thirty more. The idea was not to imitate the painting but to try to catch that essence, and the urge to rush into stitching great sweeps of color was irresistible. Needles were filled with mixed tones the way a brush gathers stray flecks from the palette, and the chair was gradually covered with bursting blooms and leaf-green tongues, creating a rich and heavy textile.

The circular cushion followed – such luminosity against the dark background. The beautiful coloring, Manet's suggestive shading, is achieved with a few simple stitches: tent, brick, long and short stitch for the silky leaves, stem stitch to suggest the dark outlining he often used.

Manet's early work had a profound effect on Monet, Sisley and Renoir – the way he produced tones as patterns of light and shade rather than color; his stunning technical virtuosity. When his work provoked such fury at the Salon, the painters who were later to become the Impressionists supported him. Being so 'notorious', he was considered their leader, but it was with reluctance – he never took part in any of their exhibitions. What drove him to seek acceptance was not the need to sell to survive (he was financially independent) but to receive recognition after the long years of hostility and rejection.

We label Manet an Impressionist, but he was nearly fifty before he adopted what we think of as a true Impressionist technique. Anyway, it is unfair to confine him to a label – it was his controversial masterpieces more than anyone's that made the leap of marrying Impressionism to mainstream art.

## Marking the canvas

Cut the canvas to size and bind the edges with tape. For a circular design, draw a circle 29cm (11½ in) in diameter on the center of the canvas with a compass. More background wool will be required for a square design.

Trace the outline (from page 149) on to the canvas with a permanent marker, centering the tracing. Follow the curved lines freely, ignoring the canvas grid. When tracing straight lines use your discretion and mark the

## STITCHING DETAILS

Finished size of design:
29cm (11½in) diameter

Yarn colors and quantities

| | DMC Laine Zephyr | | Skeins |
|---|---|---|---|
| | 200 | Cream | 3 |
| | 746 | Oatmeal | 2 |
| | 951 | Pale orange | 3 |
| | 402 | Apricot | 2 |
| | 3341 | Burnt orange | 1 |
| | 613 | Beige | 2 |
| | 358 | Pale rust | 2 |
| | 355 | Mid-rust | 1 |
| | 300 | Dark rust | 2 |
| | 320 | Jacobean green | 2 |
| | 911 | Emerald | 3 |
| | 319 | Dark green | 4 |
| | 565 | Bottle green | 3 |
| | 3052 | Sage green | 6 |

## Canvas

14-gauge white interlock
Size: 40.5cm (16in) square

## Other materials

Tapestry needle, size 20
Ruler or tape measure
Masking tape for binding the canvas
Sharp scissors for cutting the canvas
Embroidery scissors
Sharp HB pencil or fine permanent marker in
suitable color
Eraser
Compass

Before beginning to stitch, please read the
general information on page 138.

outline on the closest thread of the canvas.

If you are experienced, it is not necessary to trace the fine red lines, which show where the color on the flowers and leaves changes. If you are confident, these can be disregarded or the red lines can be put on afterwards, freehand, in a different color. A beginner may need to trace the fine lines – do this in a different color, after tracing the thick lines.

### Stitches used

TENT stitch (1), LONG and SHORT stitch (3), BRICK stitch over two threads (4), STEM stitch (7). See page 140 for stitch instructions.

### Stitching the design

Use the whole thread (4 strands) of Zephyr wool throughout. The numbers on the colored artwork refer to stitch numbers. Refer to the photo of the made up cushion and the colored artwork to see which color goes where (the arrows show the direction of the stitches). Begin by working the peonies in vertical and horizontal BRICK stitch (4) over 2 threads. The buds are in LONG and SHORT stitch (3). We have sewn the leaves in LONG and SHORT stitch (3) with some edging in STEM stitch (7). The background is TENT stitch (1).

### Finishing and making up

After sewing, the needlepoint may need to be stretched back into shape (see page 138). Then make it up into a cushion as shown on page 143.

THE FACE OF
IMPRESSIONISM

'Make portraits depict people in typical, familiar poses, being sure above all to give their faces the same kind of expression as their bodies.'

Edgar Degas

T he Impressionists painted from nature, and they painted people. If the garden scenes are top-heavy with Monet, then this section may seem biased towards Morisot. What could we do? The choice was irresolvable.

To walk through a gallery of familiar paintings is like nodding to aquaintances, a fragment of Sisley, a morsel of Morisot, canvases as appointed representatives of the painter, so well-groomed in their gilt frames. A thousand brushstrokes, a sky tarred with a storm, can be so effective in prodding memories bottled in the mind's safe-deposit, igniting the spectrum of a season you thought you'd forgotten. And what is such memory? Can two days in retrospect be the same as two months? We repeat beautiful experiences, but will the mind eventually focus on one incident, one view? One memory-jolting canvas?

The Impressionists weren't recorded or filmed, they didn't appear on chat shows. And even though they did write copious letters, the elusiveness of the person attached to the words tantalizes us and keeps the mystique intact. The Café Guerbois in the Batignolles district was where they met and discussed, and were inflamed, and sometimes doused. It is tragic for us that Herr Grundig had not yet marketed his tape recorder, because while they wrote about life, they didn't write about painting – those theories were reserved for café conversations.

In winter the daylight faded early and gaslight wasn't good for painting, so the gatherings started in the late afternoon. They sat about, the rich and the poor, discussing dreams, fearing failure, one artist arguing the need to break down tones, another advocating realism. Did they discuss hunger, insecurities? Would Manet and Degas, with their aristocratic bearing and cutting wit, have inhibited the others? Certainly as Parisians, they had little to do with rural subjects – indeed they had met while both copying a Velasquez in the Louvre. Perhaps Monet and Renoir were conscious of their lack of education and were less forceful for that reason, or was it just that Renoir had no interest in theory or controversy? He was irrepressibly light and humorous – he felt that life was for living as enjoyably as possible, and as painting was his life, that joy was inseparable from his work. Monet needed the energy of the group to recharge his strength – working in isolation can make determination falter. Sisley came less frequently to the café, and may have been too retiring to join the discussions.

Pissarro, the group guru, seems from this distance to have an almost biblical aura. However radical and anarchic his views, he was never harsh, and expressed himself with a clarity that inspired great warmth in the other Impressionist.

At the Café, *Manet, 1878.*

*Previous page: two beautiful peach-ripe Renoir girls.* The Yellow Hat *is our project and the child in the green hat was inspired by* On The Terrace, *painted in 1881.*

They discussed politics, critics, the Salon jury, materials, techniques, arguments for and against plein air, the problems of shadows – the great mystery of veiled light.

The Impressionists wanted to go further than prettified insincerity, and were adamant about truth. They were no longer painting a subject, but their true perception of the subject, probing, crystallizing. Other than Renoir, they did few portraits on commission, and instead used friends, families, sometimes people it was helpful to flatter (such as a critic), sometimes each other. Their chasing of realism meant they wielded paintbrushes both as rapiers and velvet gloves. It was not enough to show an expressive face on a posed body – the body itself, its attitudes and surroundings, had to add to the story of the moment. Such paintings, where the sitter returns the viewer's stare in a confrontational way, or a backview is as expressive as a full-faced portrait, were new. To us now, they need no qualification . . . only perhaps to add that the beautiful child in the sunlight may be all beautiful children in the sunlight.

Some of the needlepoint projects are more challenging than previous sections, others are quite straightforward. All have one thing in common: they have a grace and serenity that makes them a delight to sew. Some are on a small scale because it seems more appropriate for such intimate subjects, some are bolder and with great sweeps of stitchery, long and short stitch suggesting swathes of material, hair piled up on the head. Where stitchery is used for the focal figures to give emphasis, the background is worked simply in tent stitch. Just follow the charts and directions.

There is a quality that links these figurative pictures. The girl or woman shown is thinking of something other than the viewer, and we have a privileged glimpse into her private world.

# THE YELLOW HAT
## BY PIERRE-AUGUSTE RENOIR

Gleyre, to his pupil Renoir, with sarcasm: 'You obviously paint merely to amuse yourself', to which Renoir replied, 'Certainly. If painting didn't amuse me, I assure you I wouldn't be doing it.'

Renoir is a painter who learned at an early stage to freeze dazzling movement on canvas, with brushstrokes like thousands of irregular dancing footsteps. He indulged his subject, he indulges us, with glimpses into an epoch – and he does it with a wonderful innocence and sweetness.

Renoir's paintings went through several phases. 'One always thinks one has invented the locomotive', he said, 'until the day one realizes it doesn't work'. His work changed from being Parisian to rural when he moved with his wife and baby to the country (a relationship he kept secret for years) and later from classicism to overflowing sensuality.

This last change happened when he began painting again after the first paralyzing onslaught of his illness. The women he painted were more sensual, their poses more seductive and alluring, than at any time before. His girls and women are unique. They're cherished, luscious, tender and roly-poly, with skin that sings and would dimple if pressed. He looked constantly for the luminous combinations of tone that would give density and roundness, to make these portraits flesh and blood – almost, it seems, in direct constrast to his own wasting body. 'I like to fondle a picture, run my hand across it', he said.

## Marking the canvas and following the chart

Cut the canvas to size and bind the edges with masking tape. The design does not have to be marked out on the canvas; just follow the color chart opposite. Remember that the squares represent the canvas intersections, not the holes. Each square represents one TENT stitch.

The chart is divided into units of 10 squares by 10 squares to make it easier to follow. Before beginning to stitch, it may be helpful to mark out your canvas in similar units of 10 squares by 10 squares with an HB pencil or permanent marker in a suitable color. Also, we suggest marking the top of the canvas so that, if you turn the canvas while stitching, you will still know where the top is.

## Stitches used

TENT stitch (1), SATIN stitch (2), STEM stitch (7). For stitch instructions see page 140.

## Stitching the design

The whole thread (6 strands) of Coton Mouliné has been used throughout.

THE YELLOW HAT

## STITCHING DETAILS

Finished size of design:
17 x 17cm (6½ x 6½in)

Yarn colors and quantities
DMC Coton Mouliné Spécial          Skeins

| | | | |
|---|---|---|---|
| | 951 | Buttermilk | 1 |
| | 225 | Pastel pink | 1 |
| | 963 | Sugar pink | 1 |
| | 353 | Apricot | 1 |
| | 3776 | Pale rust | 2 |
| | 400 | Rust | 2 |
| | 898 | Dark brown | 3 |
| | 939 | Navy | 4 |
| | 977 | Orange | 1 |
| | 729 | Gold | 2 |
| | 743 | Yellow | 1 |
| | 3032 | Taupe | 2 |
| | 210 | Violet | 1 |
| | 919 | Burnt orange | 1 |
| | 666 | Red | 1 |
| | 712 | Ivory | 1 |

## Canvas

18-gauge white mono deluxe
Size: 27 x 27cm (10½ x 10½in)

## Other materials

Tapestry needle, size 22
Ruler or tape measure
Masking tape for binding the canvas
Sharp scissors for cutting the canvas
Embroidery scissors
Sharp HB pencil or fine permanent marker in
suitable color
Eraser

Before beginning to stitch, please read the
general information on page 138.

Begin in any area you wish. It might be easiest to start at the top right-hand corner, 4–5cm (1½–2in) in from the corner, working horizontally from one block of color to another.

The design can be worked entirely in TENT stitch (1) if you wish, but we have used STEM stitch (7) for outlining the hat, the girl's face, her eye and parts of her dress.

SATIN stitch (2) has been used for her lips – see the color chart and the made up cushion for the position. The outlining on the chart shows the position for STEM stitch (7). If there are spaces once you have worked the STEM stitch (7), 'fill in' with TENT stitch (1) in the relevant colors.

## Making up instructions

When the design has been sewn, the needlepoint may need to be stretched back into shape (see stretching instructions on page 138). Then make it up into a small cushion as shown on page 142, or it could be framed as a miniature picture.

# WOMAN IN HER BATH

## BY EDGAR DEGAS

'It is the human animal preoccupied with itself, like a cat licking itself. Hitherto the nude has always been shown in poses which take an audience for granted. My women are simple creatures and honest too, and are concerned with nothing except their physical occupation.'

In the Musée d'Orsay in Paris the pastels hang in a darkened room, and the dimness gives the feeling that the pictures are transient, that the fugitive colors will vanish if light is allowed in. We particularly love the *Woman in her Bath*, or to give it its full title, *Woman in her bath, sponging her leg, having forgotten her daughter's orthodontic appointment*. It is so deliciously private. For many of us the bath is a refuge, somewhere to use the sacred words 'I'm off duty' (while offspring tear at each other's throats), or a way of persuading aching joints to move in the morning. It can be the place for a candlelit 'tub à deux', or the therapeutic equivalent of passing out in a chair; a place to feel glamorous or a place to hide. Or a place to have a bath.

Pictures like this were new and outrageous – 'keyhole' pictures, where we observe solitary privacy, a woman undressing, bathing, brushing her hair, drying her feet, unaware and self-absorbed. We are voyeurs invited into an intimate scene. Degas' pastels massaged her back, coaxed her hair, soothed her shoulders – and yet it is hard to reconcile such sensuality with such a prickly man.

Degas didn't like the word Impressionist. Indeed, the list of what Degas didn't like is long. His friends' need for nature conflicted with his need for artificiality. 'I feel no need to faint in the presence of nature', he said, and when reminded that a landscape is a reflection of the soul, called it 'a reflection of my eyesight'. He loved interiors: rehearsal rooms, cafés brothels, circuses – the seamier, more basic, side of Paris life.

116

His apparent spontaneity linked him with the others, and many of his paintings are flooded with light and informality in the same way, though a little more linear, a little less shimmering. He was a realist, demonstrating that any object placed in the hands of an artist can be turned to show its significant side. And like Monet, as his sight failed, he used color with increasing flamboyance. His use of pastels is glorious, sometimes mixing them with gouache, holding them in the steam of a kettle, creating the tones of frescoes.

This little needlepoint picture was worked on fine 18-gauge canvas, hundreds of tiny stitches to the inch giving the texture of soft pastel on grained paper. Her hair is sweeping long and short stitch, the outline of her body defined with strands of fine cotton, and the overall effect is deliciously tactile.

### Marking the canvas and following the chart

Cut the canvas to size and bind the edges with masking tape. The design does not have to be marked out on the canvas; just follow the color chart on page 121. Remember that the squares represent the canvas intersections, not the holes. Each square represents one tent stitch.

The chart is divided into units of 10 squares by 10 squares to make it easier to follow. Before beginning to stitch, it may be helpful to mark out your canvas in similar units of 10 squares by 10 squares with an HB pencil or permanent marker in a suitable color. Also, we suggest marking the top of the canvas so that, if you turn the canvas while stitching, you will still know where the top is.

### Stitches used

TENT stitch (1), LONG and SHORT stitch (3), STEM stitch (7). For stitch instructions see page 140.

### Stitching the design

The whole thread (6 strands) of Coton Mouliné Spécial has been used with the exception of her hair and the outlining where 3 strands have been used.

Begin in any area you wish. It might be easiest to start at the top right-hand corner, 4–5cm (1½–2in) in from the corner, working horizontally from one block of color to another.

This design can be worked entirely in TENT stitch (1) but for a more realistic look work her hair in LONG and SHORT stitch (3) in the direction shown on the diagram. The outlining is in STEM stitch (7) – see the chart. Her face, body, arms and legs are outlined. Part of the rim of the bath and part of the chair are also outlined. If you find there are spaces once you have worked the STEM stitch (7), 'fill in' with TENT stitches in the relevant colors. If you decide to use the outlining method, this should be done at the end.

### Finishing and making up

Many needlepointers feel experienced enough to stretch and make up their needlework designs into cushions, but we always feel that a needlepoint picture should be framed by a professional, who has experience at stretching and framing needlepoint.

## STITCHING DETAILS

Finished size of design:
32 x18.5cm (12½ x 7¼in)

Yarn colors and quantities

| DMC Coton Mouliné Spécial | | | Skeins |
|---|---|---|---|
| | 822 | Stone | 4 |
| | 951 | Flesh | 1 |
| | 415 | Silver gray | 2 |
| | 503 | Almond green | 2 |
| | 452 | Heather | 2 |
| | 931 | Airforce blue | 1 |
| | 319 | Bottle green | 1 |
| | 436 | Ocher | 2 |
| | 780 | Burnt orange | 2 |
| | 400 | Rust | 2 |
| | 801 | Mid-brown | 3 |
| | 3031 | Dark brown | 2 |
| | 613 | Taupe | 3 |
| | 611 | Dark taupe | 4 |
| | 3045 | Dull gold | 2 |
| | 3787 | Dark elephant | 3 |
| } | 310 | Black | 2 |
| • | Blanc | White | 1 |
| • | 612 | Mid-taupe | 1 |

## Canvas

18-gauge white mono deluxe
Size: 42 x 28.5cm (16½ x 11¼in)

## Other materials

Tapestry needle, size 22
Ruler or tape measure
Masking tape for binding the canvas
Sharp scissors for cutting the canvas
Embroidery scissors
Sharp HB pencil or fine permanent marker in
suitable color
Eraser

*Lines on the diagram show the stitches on her hair.*

# DANCER REHEARSING

## BY EDGAR DEGAS

'If someone said I had lost my mind, don't you think I'd be pleased? What use is my mind? Granted that it enables me to hail a bus and pay my fare. But once I am inside my studio, what use is my mind? I have my model, my pencil, my paper, my paints. My mind doesn't interest me.'

Even if not an enthusiast of ballet performance, it is the contradictions of ballet that are fascinating. That something so graceful and apparently effortless can be achieved only through punishing practice, defying all normal boundaries of physical frailty, is as incongruous as petals cast in iron. And it is the concentration of the dancers' inward-looking world that Degas usually shows us, not the public face of performance, the stage smile. And how different these swans are from the three-year-old uncoordinates in podgy pink, learning their positions in the church hall, with Mrs Bayliss at the piano, the damp smell of wellingtons, a row of beaming mothers and the caretaker waiting to lock up.

More than half Degas' output is of the ballet and most of those are backstage scenes or rehearsal rooms. The dancers are quite inaccessible to us, both fragile and earthed. It is easy to imagine Degas, an austere fixture in the rehearsal rooms, observing with a surgeon's eye. He had a reputation for mysogeny, for coldness and sarcasm, he could be harsh, unreasonable and obstinate, and felt himself 'so badly made, so poorly tooled, sulky with everyone and with myself'. Not a laugh a minute, our Edgar. Yet it seems he was adored by the dancers he drew, and treated them like his children.

Degas' work looks so spontaneous, but most of it was done in the studio, carefully reconstructed from sketches he had made. He wrote 'Never was an art less spontaneous than my own. A painting is something which requires as much trickery as the perpetuation of a crime'. His studio was equipped with bathtubs, screens, furniture, to create bath, brothel or boudoir. He lived alone, in two apartments one above the other, looked after by his general factotum Zoë. There were drawings and paintings everywhere, the walls full, stacked on the floors. Had he not hung so many he could have fulfilled his lifelong dream to paint on walls.

As time went by, Degas chose models of, shall we say, a certain age and physique, a little beyond their best – to be blunt, having the kind of squidginess of limb that makes many of us convinced the mirror is distorted. He drew them rapidly, memorably, creating images with bare economy of line, freezing ephemeral gestures: the tying of a shoelace, adjusting a shoulder strap, involvement, isolation, the bustle of the group, the stillness of the singular.

## Marking the canvas

Cut the canvas to size and bind the edges with masking tape. Trace the outline (from pages 156–7) on to the canvas with a permanent marker, centering the tracing. Follow the curved lines freely, ignoring the canvas grid. When tracing straight lines use your discretion and mark the outline on the closest thread of the canvas.

If you are experienced it is not necessary to trace the fine red lines, which are a guide to show where the colors change. If your are confident, these can be disregarded or the red lines can be put on afterwards, freehand, in a different color. A beginner may need to trace the red lines – do this in a different color, after you have finished tracing the thick lines.

## Stitches used

TENT stitch (1), SATIN stitch (2), LONG and SHORT stitch (3), CONTINUOUS MOSAIC stitch (5), STEM stitch (7), and ENCROACHING LONG and SHORT stitch (8).

## Stitching the design

Two threads of Medicis wool have been used throughout except for the outline around her profile, back, arms, body and the fine dark brown lines on her skirt where one thread has been used.

The thread has been mixed in certain areas and this is indicated on the color key. Where it is mixed, use one strand of each color.

The instructions on page 140 will show you how to do the stitches. The numbers on the colored artwork refer to the stitch numbers. The arrows show the direction. Refer to the photograph of the made up picture and the colored artwork to show you which color goes where. Remember, this is a guide, do not be restricted by it and feel free to experiment.

All outlining is in STEM stitch (7). Her hair is in LONG and SHORT stitch (3). Her face, back, arms, hands, legs, feet and shoes are in TENT stitch (1); the bodice of her dress is also TENT stitch (1). The ribbon around her neck and the bow on her dress are in diagonal SATIN stitch (2). Her skirt is in ENCROACHING LONG and SHORT stitch (8). The floor is in CONTINUOUS MOSAIC stitch (5) and the wall is in TENT stitch (1).

## Finishing and making up

Many needlepointers feel experienced enough to stretch and make up their needlework designs into cushions, but we always feel that a needlepoint picture should be framed by a professional, who has experience at stretching and framing needlepoint.

### STITCHING DETAILS

Finished size of design:
21 x 32cm (8¼ x 12½in)

Yarn colors and quantities

| DMC Broder Medicis | | | Skeins |
|---|---|---|---|
| | 8838 | Brown | 2 |
| | 8515 | Cream | 5 |
| | 8109 | Beige | 5 |
| | 8501 | Pale beige | 2 |
| | Blanc | White | 1 |
| | 8381 | Pale gray | 2 |
| | 8508 | Gray blue | 2 |
| | 8930 | Marine blue | 1 |
| | 8164 | Apricot | 1 |
| | 8105 | Terracotta | 2 |

Mixed colors

| | 8109/8105 |
|---|---|

### Canvas

18-gauge white mono interlock
Size: 30.5 x 42cm (12 x 16½in)

### Other materials

Tapestry needle, size 22
Ruler or tape measure
Masking tape for binding the canvas
Sharp scissors for cutting the canvas
Embroidery scissors
Sharp HB pencil or fine permanent marker

# LADY AT HER TOILETTE

## BY BERTHE MORISOT

'It seems to me that I am about the only one without any pettiness of character: this makes up for my inferiority as a painter.'

As women, we live our lives in stages. There are the childhood years, the loving and the breeding, growing to encompass responsibilities, disappointments, compromises. We often leave ourselves in suspension – a shelved person to be re-met when outside demands lessen. Perhaps only in middle age can the crystallization of what has gone before take place. For most of us the stages happen imperceptibly, one naturally superceding the last. We assume we won't forget, but we do, if not the events then the sensations. Choices are marked with the branched diviner's twig, and later with the superb wisdom of hindsight. We have photographs, but what do they say about the photographer? And the internal photographs we have are victims of fading as much as sepia prints.

Paintings can be different. Looking at Berthe Morisot's paintings, it is possible to sense her emotions as she passed through different phases of her life: her own voice speaks as clearly as her subject. Mothers and daughters: they play hide and seek, they catch butterflies, the child offers a posy of flowers, long grasses, long summers. A sitter looks out from her portrait with affection or with restraint, or gazes absently through a window, into middle age, into middle distance.

Her brushstrokes look random, flicking freely in every direction, truly impressionistic with little solid form, just glowing dashes of color that

STITCHING DETAILS

Only an experienced needlepointer should attempt this project – it is not for a beginner.

Finished size of design:
25.5 x31cm (10 x 12¼in)

Yarn colors and quantities

| DMC Laine Zephyr | | | Skeins |
|---|---|---|---|
| | 928 | Dull blue | 3 |
| | 762 | Pale blue | 2 |
| | 3010 | Pale green | 4 |
| | 422 | Yellow ocher | 2 |
| | 613 | Beige | 2 |
| | 408 | Cinnamon | 2 |
| | 840 | Chocolate | 3 |
| | 934 | Dark brown | 2 |
| | 224 | Dusky pink | 2 |

| DMC Coton Mouliné Spécial | | | Skeins |
|---|---|---|---|
| | Blanc | White | 2 |
| | 809 | Bright blue | 1 |
| | 775 | Pale blue | 3 |
| | 712 | Flesh | 4 |
| | 842 | Mid-flesh | 3 |
| | 841 | Dark flesh | 2 |
| | 758 | Apricot | 2 |
| | 966 | Peppermint green | 2 |

Mixed colors

| | |
|---|---|
| • | 712/842 |
| • | 841/842 |
| • | 758/842 |

Canvas

14-gauge white interlock
Size: 36 x 41cm (14 x 16in)

Other materials

Tapestry needle, size 20
Ruler or tape measure
Masking tape for binding the canvas
Sharp scissors for cutting the canvas
Embroidery scissors
Sharp HB pencil or fine permanent marker in suitable color
Eraser

Before beginning to stitch, please read the general information on page 138.

speak with great clarity. The paintings don't stop at the edge of the canvas, they wrap around and behind us, and gently include us. We are invited into the world of the bourgeoisie by a painter of elegance and determination.

*Lady at her Toilette* is a glorious painting, glowing with light. A private moment, a turned back, she adjusts her hair in the mirror. Her skin is worked in tones of cotton, little flat stitches built up into blended shades; her gown in sweeping strokes of the same cotton, all contrasting with the wool background.

When Morisot was 16, she and her sisters had drawing lessons arranged by their mother so that they could give their father drawings for his birthday. Mme Morisot had no idea what floodgates she was opening. She was told that such talent would make her daughters painters, which in their social milieu 'could be revolutionary, even catastrophic'. Morisot's sister Edma, also a greatly gifted painter, married and made the difficult choice of giving up art to be wife and mother. This was the customary decision – Morisot's commitment to painting was the more unusual.

In the 1870s there were increasing numbers of women becoming artists, fighting society's pressure that they conform. Social propriety prevented

Morisot from joining the café discussions with the other Impressionists, even though she knew most of them. She could only meet Manet and Degas, who shared similar haute-bourgeois backgrounds, at salons held by her parents or friends. One of the great attractions of plein-air painting was that there was no need for a chaperone.

Morisot wrote to Edma, 'Men incline to believe that they fill all of one's life, but as for me, I think that no matter how much affection a woman has for her husband, it is not easy for her to break with a life of work. Affection is a very fine thing, on condition that there is something besides to fill one's days.' Needlepoint, possibly.

## Marking the canvas

Cut the canvas to size and bind the edges with masking tape. This is a combined chart and artwork design. Trace the outline (from pages 154–5) on to the canvas with a permanent marker, using the straight outline as a guide for the edge of the design. Follow the curved lines freely, ignoring the canvas grid. Trace the straight edge. When tracing straight lines use your discretion and mark the outline on the closest thread of the canvas.

If you are experienced it is not necessary to trace the fine red lines, which are a guide to show where the colors change. These red lines can be disregarded or can be put on afterwards, freehand, in a different color. A beginner may find it easier to follow the design by tracing the fine lines – do this with a permanent marker in a different color, after you have finished tracing the thick lines.

## Stitches used

TENT stitch (1), SATIN stitch (2), LONG and SHORT stitch (3), STEM stitch (7), and ENCROACHING LONG and SHORT stitch (8).

The instructions on page 140 will show you how to do the stitches. The numbers on the colored artwork refer to the stitch numbers. Look at the photograph of the made up picture and the colored artwork to show you which color goes where (the arrows show the directions of the stitches). Remember, this is a guide, do not be restricted by it and feel free to experiment.

## Stitching the design

*Background*: Wool and cotton have been used separately in this design. Where wool is specified use the whole thread of Zephyr wool (4 strands) and where cotton is specified use the whole thread of Coton Mouliné Spécial (6 strands).

*The figure* (including her dress and hair): Wool has been used for her hair, the choker, part of her dress and some outlining – use 2 strands of Zephyr wool in these places. An explanation for how to split the wool appears on page 139. Where cotton has been specified use the whole thread of Coton Mouliné Spécial (6 strands). The cotton has been mixed on the flesh in some areas and this is indicated on the color key and the colored artwork. Where the cotton is mixed use three strands of each color (6 strands equals one thread).

### Following the chart

When you have completed tracing the figure, follow the color chart and 'fill in' the background. Remember that the squares represent the canvas intersections, not the holes. Each square represents one TENT stitch.

The chart is divided into units of 10 squares by 10 squares to make it easier to follow. Before beginning to stitch the background, it may be helpful to mark out your canvas in similar units of 10 squares by 10 squares with an HB pencil or permanent marker in a suitable color.

### Stitching the background

The background is worked entirely in TENT stitch (1). Begin in any area you wish. It might be easiest to start at the top right-hand corner working horizontally in blocks of color, filling in the background around the figure and then working the areas of flesh. Do not be concerned if you have to compensate by leaving out some stitches as everyone will trace and stitch the figure in a slightly different way.

### Stitching the figure

Stitch the lady's hair in LONG and SHORT stitch (3) in the direction of the arrows. Her dress is worked in ENCROACHING LONG and SHORT stitch (8) with some outlining in STEM stitch (7). Her choker is in VERTICAL SATIN stitch (2) edged in STEM stitch (7). Her face, arms and back are worked in TENT stitch (1) with some outlining in STEM stitch (7) and her features are also in STEM stitch (7) where indicated.

### Finishing and making up

Many needlepointers feel experienced enough to stretch and make up their needlework designs into cushions, but we always feel that a needlepoint picture should be framed by a professional, who has experience at stretching and framing needlepoint.

# CHILD ON A STOOL
## FROM *THE STORY* BY BERTHE MORISOT

'The young Morisot girls are charming. It's a pity they're not men.'

Edouard Manet

There is a precious time in childhood, before outside influences intervene, when a child will sit and listen to a story, transported, entranced. The eyes are fixed, the mind a silver screen, belief is total. Come with me, you say, I will take you to magic places, and the willing hand puts itself in yours and the story begins. The painting that inspired our needlepoint picture is called *La Fable*, the story. Outside our picture is a woman, perhaps the child's mother, weaving webs; the child sits on a stool, in the way that only a five-year-old sits on a stool, so rapt, teddy clutched. Those fortunate enough to have known such children will be able to feel the flesh of that elbow, the wispy nape of disobedient hair, the body stilled with attention. It will soon be time for bread and chocolate, meanwhile there is trust, and wonder, and the ability to fly.

Berthe Morisot is our favorite of the Impressionist group, perhaps her choice of subject is closest to our hearts. Her pictures are both intimate and confrontational, her domestic scenes simple, we eavesdrop on conversations; she recorded the core of domestic intimacy. These pictures are quiet, and luminous – a spotlight guides us to exactly what she wanted to share.

STITCHING DETAILS

Finished size of design:
22 x 32cm (8½ x 12½in)

Yarn colors and quantities

| DMC Laine Zephyr | | | Skeins |
|---|---|---|---|
| | 945 | Pale peach | 2 |
| | 402 | Orange | 2 |
| | 358 | Terracotta | 1 |
| | 3043 | Lavender | 1 |
| | 224 | Dusky pink | 1 |
| | 3042 | Lilac | 1 |
| | 799 | Baby blue | 1 |
| | 422 | Sand | 2 |
| | 413 | Charcoal | 1 |
| | 613 | Beige | 4 |
| | 420 | Cinnamon | 1 |
| | 612 | Brown | 3 |
| | 611 | Dark brown | 1 |
| | 373 | Duck egg blue | 2 |
| | 772 | Lime | 2 |
| | 368 | Almond | 2 |
| | 989 | Jade | 1 |
| | 522 | Jacobean green | 2 |
| | 936 | Olive | 3 |
| | 895 | Bottle | 3 |
| | 200 | Cream | 2 |

Mixed colors

| | |
|---|---|
| | 613/612 |
| | 373/200 |
| | 945/402 |

Canvas

14-gauge white interlock
Size: 32 x 42cm (12½ x 16½in)

Other materials

Tapestry needle, size 20
Ruler or tape measure
Masking tape for binding the canvas
Sharp scissors for cutting the canvas
Embroidery scissors
Sharp HB pencil or fine permanent marker in suitable color
Eraser

Before beginning to stitch, please read the general information on page 138.

At twenty-three she submitted works to the official Salon, which were accepted and admired. She met the artist Fantin-Latour and through him the rest of the group. Her relationship with Manet was as mutually enriching as Cassatt's with Degas – he admired her talent and beauty, she posed for him frequently and memorably. She encouraged him to paint outdoors, and to lighten his palette; he influenced her portraits. She continued to exhibit at the Salon for the next nine years.

The tenth year, 1874, was a good year. Mrs Churchill had Winston, Verdi introduced his Requiem, Stanley went 'Into Africa', and Berthe Morisot married Manet's brother, Eugène. It was also the year of the first Impressionist Exhibition – Morisot was a mainstay of these group shows, exhibiting at all except the year her daughter Julie was born.

By today's expectations, Julie was a dutiful daughter, though in her diaries frequently vowed to 'be nicer to Maman' – the familiar universal

intention. Every stage of her growing up was recorded on canvas by her mother. The children of painters become used to this – sometimes the mood is too beautiful to interrupt, the child is instructed in a whisper not to move, the painter feels for charcoal, burnt umber, paper, without averting the gaze from a perfectly cupped chin, or fall of fairy hair. Those poor children, making the mistake of choosing such parents.

## Marking the canvas

Cut the canvas to size and bind the edges with masking tape. This is a combined chart and artwork design. Trace the outline (from page 145) on to the canvas with a permanent marker, using the straight outline as a guide for the edge of the design. Follow the curved lines freely, ignoring the canvas grid. Trace the straight edge. When tracing straight lines use your discretion and mark the outline on the closest thread of the canvas.

If you are experienced it is not necessary to trace the fine red lines, which are a guide to show where the colors change. These red lines can be disregarded or can be put on afterwards, freehand, in a different color. A beginner may find it easier to follow the design by tracing the fine lines – do this with a permanent marker in a different color, after you have finished tracing the thick lines.

## Stitches used

TENT stitch (1), Reversed TENT stitch (1a) ◥, SATIN stitch (2), LONG and SHORT stitch (3), BRICK stitch (over two threads) (4), and STEM stitch (7).

## Stitching the child

Use the whole thread of Zephyr wool (4 strands) with the following exceptions when 2 strands are used: all outlining, the cuff on the girl's sleeve and her shoes. An explanation for how to split the wool appears on page 139.

The wool has been mixed in certain areas and this is indicated on the color key. Where it is mixed, use two strands of each color.

The instructions on page 140 will show you how to do the stitches. The numbers on the colored artwork refer to the stitch numbers. Look at the photograph of the made up picture and the colored artwork to show you which color goes where. Remember, this is a guide, do not be restricted by it and feel free to experiment.

Begin by stitching the girl's hair in LONG and SHORT stitch (3) edged in STEM stitch (7). Her hair ribbon is worked in SATIN stitch (2). All outlining is in STEM stitch (7). The cuff on her dress is in SATIN stitch (2) and her teddy is in vertical BRICK stitch (4) over two threads. Her dress, stockings, face and arm are in TENT stitch (1) outlined in STEM stitch (7). Her shoes are in SATIN stitch (2), outlined in STEM stitch (7).

### Following the chart

When you have completed stitching the child follow the color chart and 'fill in' the background. Remember that the squares represent the canvas intersections, not the holes. Each square represents one TENT stitch.

The chart is divided into units 10 squares by 10 squares to make it easier to follow. Before beginning to stitch the background, it may be helpful to mark out your canvas in similar units of 10 squares by 10 squares with an HB pencil or permanent marker in a suitable color.

### Stitching the background

The background is worked entirely in TENT stitch (1) with the stool and trellis in reversed TENT stitch (1a) and this is indicated on the color chart. Begin in any area you wish. It might be easiest to start by 'filling in' the stitches on the edge of the figure and work outwards. Do not be concerned if you have to compensate by leaving out some stitches, as everyone will trace the figure in a slightly different way.

### Finishing and making up

Many needlepointers feel experienced enough to stretch and make up their needlework designs into cushions, but we always fell that a needlepoint picture should be framed by a professional, who has experience at stretching and framing needlepoint.

# GENERAL INFORMATION

## MARKING THE CANVAS

Always leave a border of at least 5cm (2in) of unstitched canvas around all the edges of the design for stretching purposes.

When marking out a canvas into squares of 10 threads by 10 threads, you should use a permanent marker, an HB pencil or a water-erasable marking pen.

To trace a design through on to canvas, place the canvas on top of the drawing and mark the outline with a permanent marker, an HB pencil or a water-erasable marking pen. The patterns for tracing have been given a heavy outline so that you can trace directly from the page if you wish, but if you don't want to risk spoiling the book, draw the design on to tracing paper first, using a black marker.

A design can also be painted on to canvas in oil or acrylic paint, using a soft fine brush. Ensure that whatever medium you use is waterproof as it would be disastrous if the color ran when the work was dampened for stretching.

## STITCHING

The colors shown on the charts are stronger than the actual yarn colors to make them easier to see. The corresponding yarns are given in the color keys.

When working from a chart, start at the top right-hand corner 5cm (2in) in from the edge. Stitch horizontally from one block of color to another.

We suggest you use the basket-weave method on a large area of tent stitch as it does not put a strain on the canvas and a more even tension is achieved.

When working a design using stitchery, it is advisable to work the outline first, then the design and finally the background, but there are no hard-and-fast rules. Use compensating stitches (small filling-in stitches) where necessary.

White yarn should be left until last to keep it clean. Don't let the ends of other colors get caught into the stitches.

## WORKING METHODS

We suggest you use a frame when stitching, but this is a personal choice. There is no question that the finish is better and a more even tension is achieved, but if you are more comfortable working without a frame, that is fine. Just try not to pull too tightly.

Some people need a thimble, and at some point in your needlepoint career you may well need a seam unpicker!

Cut your tapestry wool into lengths of approximately 75cm (30in); cut stranded cotton, coton perlé, gold thread and crewel wool into 38–50cm (15–20in) lengths.

To begin, knot the wool temporarily on the front of the canvas about 2.5cm (1in) from where you want to start, in the direction in which you will be working. As you work your canvas, the stitches on the back will anchor the 2.5cm (1in) thread. When you reach the knot, cut it off and the thread should be quite secure. When you re-thread your needle to continue sewing the same area, there is no need to knot the wool; simply run the needle through the work on the underside. To finish, do the same in reverse.

Keep the back of the canvas tidy for two simple reasons. Firstly, having lots of ends hanging at the back can eventually make it difficult to get your needle through the canvas. Secondly, the work will lie flatter when it is made up. So cut your threads short when you have anchored them.

## CARING FOR FINISHED PIECES

Just as we would never cover an oil painting with glass, we never use glass on a framed needlepoint. They deserve to be enjoyed as textured and interesting pieces, not flattened and diminished behind glass.

To keep needlepoint pictures clean, just flick over with a feather duster. Ideally, needlepoint should not be in a smoky atmosphere – and after all, stitching is an excellent way of cutting down on smoking, and eating for that matter.

Needlepoint can be Scotch-Guarded and we strongly recommend that you do not wash it. If it gets dirty, take it to a good dry cleaner's instead.

## FINISHING AND MAKING UP

Many needlepointers feel experienced enough to stretch and make up their needlework designs into cushions, bags, stool tops and a variety of other items, but we always feel that a needlepoint picture should be framed by a professional who has particular experience in stretching and framing needlepoint.

If you would like to stretch your own needlepoint before making up, use the following method.

### Stretching

Materials needed:
Blotting paper
Clean flat board
Tacks, staples or drawing pins
The needlepoint must be 'square' before framing or making into a cushion, bag, stool top, etc. If it is out of square, lightly dampen or spray it and leave for a few minutes to soften the canvas. Gently pull square and then pin out, right side down, on to blotting paper on a clean flat board. Use tacks, staples or drawing pins and pin outside the sewn surface. Do not strain the canvas too tightly or the needlepoint will dry with a scalloped edge. When the needlepoint is thoroughly dry (this may take two or three days), remove it from the board.

### Making Up

Instructions are given on pages 142–144 for making your needlepoint into cushions, belts, placemats, etc. Firm cotton, chintz, brocade and moire are all easy fabrics to work with for cushion backing. Medium-weight velvet also makes an attractive backing but is a little more difficult for beginners to handle. We don't recommend upholstery velvet, which is very thick.

Ready-made cushion pads can be bought in various sizes. For a flat effect, use a pad the same size as the needlepoint cover. We prefer a plumper cushion – use a pad 5cm (2in) larger than the cover. Boxed cushions should have a pad with a gusset. Ease the pad into the cushion cover gently to avoid putting any strain on the zipper, pushing it carefully into the corners to fill them out.

### ADAPTING CHARTS AND ARTWORK

When following a chart, you can easily change the gauge of canvas you choose. If you decide on 10 canvas where we have suggested 18 canvas, remember that the design will be almost twice the size. It is important to change the yarn to a more suitable thickness, and also the needle size. Likewise, if we suggest 10 canvas and you use 18 canvas, the size of the finished needlepoint will be almost half the size. Artwork can be reduced in size or enlarged on a photocopier.

If you are adapting a photograph, do a tracing of it first and have the tracing

CANVAS/YARN/NEEDLE CHART

| Canvas<br><br>holes to<br>the inch | Needle<br>size | Laine Colbert<br>(tapestry wool) | Laine Zephyr<br>(Zephyr wool)<br><br>4 strands to<br>the thread | Laine Medicis<br>(Medicis<br>crewel wool) | Coton Perlé<br>(Pearl cotton)<br><br>No. 3<br>No. 5 | Coton Mouliné<br>(stranded cotton)<br><br>6 strands to<br>the thread |
|---|---|---|---|---|---|---|
| 7 | 16 | 2 threads | – | – | – | – |
| 10 | 18 | 1 thread | 1½ threads<br>(i.e. 6 strands) | 4/5 threads | – | 9/12 strands |
| 12 | 18<br>or 20 | 1 thread | 1 thread | 4 threads | No. 3<br>1 thread | 9 strands |
| 14 | 20 | – | 1 thread | 3 threads | No. 3<br>1 thread | 6/9 strands |
| 16 | 22 | – | ¾ thread<br>(ie 3 strands) | 2/3 threads | No. 5 – 1/2 threads<br>No. 3 – 1 thread | 6 strands |
| 18 | 22 | – | ½ thread<br>(ie 2 strands) | 2 threads | No. 5 – 1 | 4/6 strands |

This chart is a guide. The amount of strands/threads you use depends on the stitches, i.e. tent stitch uses fewer strands/threads than satin stitch.

enlarged or reduced. Then transfer the design on to your canvas as described in Marking the Canvas (left). An example is the Peony cushion project on page 107. The project is on 14-gauge canvas. We have shown the same design worked on 7-gauge canvas for the Peony chair. The canvas was stitched using the thread double.

The chart above will help if you decide to change the size of the project.

## YARN

We have used DMC yarn in all our projects and the following explanation will help in determining which yarn to choose in your project.

### DMC Laine Colbert (tapestry wool)

A high quality, hard-wearing non-divisible 4-ply wool available in 8 metre (8¾ yard) skeins or 20 gm (¾ oz) 38 metre (42 yard) hanks.

### DMC Laine Zephyr (Zephyr wool)

A divisible 4-strand wool. Two, three or four strands can be used. Available in 8 metre (8¾ yard) skeins. To split the wool in two (i.e. 2 strands in each thread) hold one end of the thread with your teeth and, beginning in the middle, split the thread with your hands, pulling gently and slowly apart.

### DMC Laine Medicis (Medicis crewel wool)

A fine quality crewel wool. Perfect for mixing. Can be used singly or in one, two and three strands. Available in 25 metre (27 yard) skeins.

### DMC Coton Perlé (pearl cotton)

It is available in two thicknesses: No. 5 and No. 3. This is a highly mercerised twisted non-divisible thread available in 25 metre (27 yard) skeins.

### DMC Coton Mouliné (stranded cotton)

This stranded cotton is a brilliant 6-strand divisible thread available in 8 metre (8¾ yard) skeins.

### DMC Fil Or Clair (gold thread)

A shiny gold metallic thread. Use singly or as many strands as you need to cover the canvas. Treat the yarn gently – do not pull too tightly.

# WORKING THE STITCHES

The following stitches are used in the needlepoint projects:

## 1 TENT STITCH
## 1a REVERSED TENT STITCH

TENT stitch, which forms a fine background of short slanting stitches, can be worked in a number of different ways. CONTINENTAL TENT stitch (A) is worked *horizontally* across the canvas. Work from right to left. At the end of the row, turn the canvas upside down and work the next row, again from right to left. In REVERSED TENT stitch, the stitches simply slant in the other direction. VERTICAL TENT stitch should only be used for single *vertical* lines, e.g. outlining.
BASKETWEAVE (B) is worked *diagonally* from the top-right hand corner without turning the canvas. This is the best stitch to use on larger areas of background as it does not distort the canvas as CONTINENTAL tends to

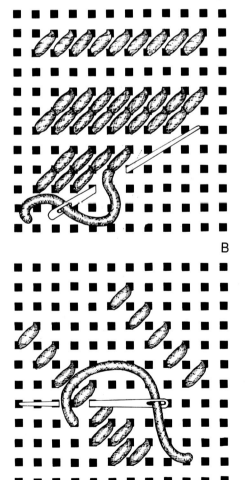

A

B

## 2 SATIN STITCH

This is an easy and versatile stitch, good for 'filling in' and wonderful in borders as numerous different patterns can be formed. It is also the basis for many other stitches. SATIN stitch (A) is made up of straight stitches set close together. Here the stitches are shown first worked diagonally in both directions, then worked *vertically* and then *horizontally*. It can also radiate out from the center (B).

A

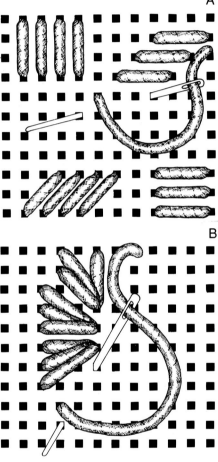

B

## 3 LONG and SHORT STITCH

LONG AND SHORT stitch is a form of SATIN stitch more commonly used in embroidery. It is so called due to the varying lengths of the stitches. It is useful on areas too large or irregular to be covered by SATIN stitch – perfect for flower petals as it can follow each curve. In the first row of LONG AND SHORT stitch, the stitches are alternately long and short and follow the outline. **The stitches in the following rows are of similar lengths** and fit in to the previous row. For a smoother effect, split the thread of the previous stitch.

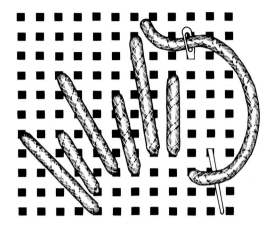

## 4 BRICK STITCH

BRICK stitch consists of a series of straight stitches taken over two or four canvas threads and laid in staggered rows like bricks. The stitch can be worked horizontally or vertically, and makes an excellent background stitch.
The top line of stitching shows how each row is worked over four threads of canvas with a space of two threads in between. The lower line of stitching shows how the next row begins two threads lower down and the stitches interlock neatly.
Work the first row from right to left, the second row from left to right, and so on. Do not turn the canvas.

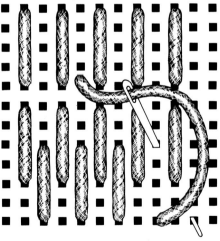

## 5 CONTINUOUS MOSAIC STITCH

CONTINUOUS MOSAIC stitch is an interesting background stitch which gives the impression of woven straw.
The stitch is worked in diagonal rows which can slant either from right to left or from left to right as you wish.
Work the stitch *diagonally* over one and

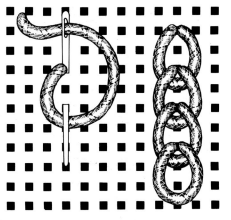

## 7 STEM STITCH

This is useful for flower stems or outlining. Work from left to right, using stitches of a similar length. Each stitch overlaps the previous one.

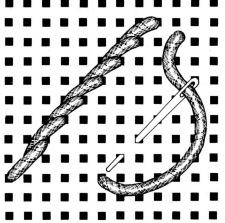

## 8 ENCROACHING LONG and SHORT STITCH

As with LONG and SHORT stitch, it is so called because of the varying lengths of the stitches.

This stitch can be worked vertically or horizontally. For an 'encroaching' look tuck it slightly behind the last stitch, into a previously 'covered' hole.

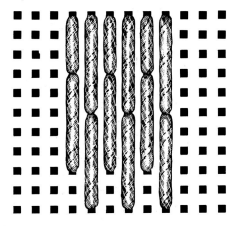

two threads of canvas. The second row butts up to the first – the small stitch interlocks neatly with the larger stitch. Do not pull the thread tightly as this will distort the canvas. Work rows alternately upwards and downwards.

## 6 CHAIN STITCH

When CHAIN stitch is worked in close rows, it makes a texture rather like knitting. Work *vertically* from the top down. To make a *horizontal* row, give the canvas a quarter turn so that the top is at the side, then work the row *vertically*. To begin a row, bring the thread through at the top and, holding the thread down with your left thumb, insert the needle into the same hole and bring it out two canvas threads lower down. Keeping the thread under the needle, pull the needle through the loop. To continue, hold the thread down, put the needle into the same hole and bring it out two canvas threads down. With thread under needle, pull the needle through the loop. To finish a row, work a tiny straight stitch into the same hole to anchor the loop. Work rows two canvas threads apart.

141

# MAKING UP INSTRUCTIONS

## SMALL CUSHION WITH A BRAIDED INSET
Illustrated on page 111
**Materials**
0.35m (14in) fabric 122cm (48in) wide
Approx 2m (2¼yd) braid
Pins
Kapok or terylene filling

1  Cut two pieces of fabric 28 x 28cm (11 x 11in).
2  Cut away excess canvas from the needlepoint leaving 1.2cm (½in) of unsewn canvas.
3  Tack the needlepoint to one of the fabric pieces making sure it is central. Applique by using the zig-zag stitch on your machine set on a close setting. Trim away any of the excess canvas that will show under the braid.
4  Mark a chalk line across this piece of fabric following the line of the finished needlepoint. Pin or tack on the braid down each side and machine into place. Repeat for the top and bottom.
5  Tack or pin the cushion backing to the front, right sides together, taking a 1.2cm (½in) turning and machine into place leaving an 18cm (7in) opening. Turn through to the right side and stuff with a polyester filling of your choice.

## CUSHION WITH TWISTED CORD TRIM
**Materials**
0.5m (⅝yd) fabric 122cm (48in) wide or remnant slightly larger than cushion size
Zipper 8cm (3in) shorter than height of finished cushion
Twisted cord 10cm (4in) longer than the measurement around the cushion
Pins
Clear adhesive tape

1  Stretch the needlepoint back to its original shape and cut away any excess canvas, leaving 1.2cm (½in) of unsewn canvas for turning.
2  Cut out the cushion back to the same size as the canvas, adding 5cm (2in) to the width measurement for the zipper seam. Fold the fabric in half from side to side and cut along the crease to form the zipper opening.
3  At each end of the zipper opening, stitch a 5cm (2in) seam, taking 2.5cm (1in) turnings. Press seam open. Sew in

the zipper (fig.1). Remember to leave it open to turn the cushion through.

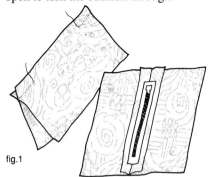
fig.1

4  Tack or pin the fabric to the needlepoint right sides together. Machine around the edge of the needlepoint, leaving a 2.5cm (1in) opening at the bottom. Double stitch or overlock the seams. Turn the cushion to the right side through the zipper opening.
5  Sew on the cord by hand starting from the opening at the bottom and leaving a small 'tail' (fig.2). (Before cutting the cord, wrap the ends with adhesive tape to prevent them fraying.) Join the cord by weaving the ends together and securing with a few stitches. Wrap the join with adhesive tape before cutting away any excess cord. Tuck the ends into the opening and neaten by sewing in.

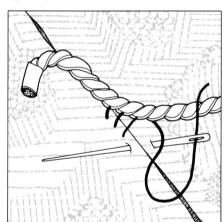
fig.2

## CUSHION WITH FRINGED EDGING
Illustrated on page 55
**Materials**
0.5m (⅝yd) fabric 122cm (48in) wide or remnant slightly larger than cushion size
Zipper 8cm (3in) shorter than height of finished cushion
Fringe 7.5cm (3in) longer than the

measurement around the cushion
Pins
Clear adhesive tape

1–4  Follow steps 1–4 of Cushion with twisted cord trim.
5  Sew on the fringe by hand as close to the needlepoint as possible. Turn under the raw ends and butt together.

## CUSHION WITH TWISTED CORD AND LOOPS AT EACH CORNER
Illustrated on page 68
**Materials**
0.5m (⅝yd) fabric 122cm (48in) wide or remnant slightly larger than cushion size
Zipper 8cm (3in) shorter than height of finished cushion
Twisted cord approx 56cm (22in) longer than the measurement around the cushion
Pins
Clear adhesive tape

1–4  Follow steps 1–4 of Cushion with twisted cord trim.
5  Sew on the cord by hand starting from the opening at the bottom and leaving a small 'tail', as in step 5 of Cushion with twisted cord trim. Sew to the corner and make a loop. Secure the loop with a few stitches. Repeat when you reach the other three corners. (Before cutting the cord, wrap the ends with adhesive tape.)
6  Join the cord by weaving the ends together and securing with a few stitches. Wrap the join with adhesive tape before cutting away any excess cord. Tuck the ends into the opening and neaten by sewing in.

## CUSHION WITH TWO NEEDLEPOINT PANELS
Illustrated on page 19
**Materials**
0.5m (⅝yd) fabric 122cm (48in) wide
30cm (12in) zipper
2.75m (3yd) trimming of your choice
Pins

1  Stretch the panels back to the original shape.
2  Cut the backing and the panels as plan above (fig.1).
3  Fold the fabric in half from side to side and cut along the crease to form the zipper opening. At each end of the zipper opening stitch a 4cm (1½in) seam, taking

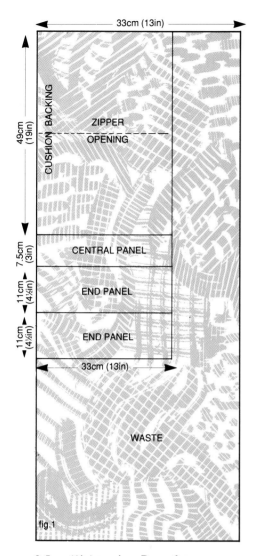

fig.1

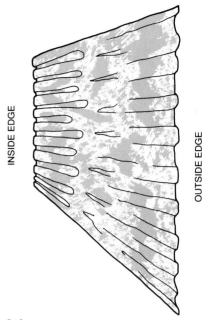

fig.2

Zipper 8cm (3in) shorter than height of cushion
2.75m (3yd) cord
Pins

1 Stretch the needlepoint back to the original shape.
2 Cut out the fabric following the cutting plan (fig.1).
3 Fold the fabric in half from side to side and cut along the crease to form the zipper opening. At each end of the zipper opening stitch a 4cm (1½in) seam, taking a 2.5cm (1in) turning. Press the seam open and sew in the zipper.
4 Cut out a paper pattern 52cm (20½in) in diameter. Pin the circular paper pattern to the cushion backing and cut out.
5 Join the borders together to make a long strip. Press the seams open.
6 Gather both sides of the border, making the inside edge much fuller than the outside edge. At this stage it should look like fig.2.
7 Cut away the excess canvas, leaving 1.2cm (½in) of unsewn canvas for turning.
8 Pin or tack the inside of the border to the needlepoint right sides together, leaving a 2.5cm (1in) opening for the cord, pushing in more fullness if necessary. Join the ends together and then

machine into place, keeping close to the finished needlepoint. At this stage it should look like fig.3. The outside gathers can be adjusted if necessary.
9 Tack the backing to the cushion right sides together leaving a 2.5cm (1in) opening for the cord. Machine into place. Overlock or double stitch the seams. Turn to the right side through the zipper opening.
10 Sew on the cord by hand, as in step 5 of Cushion with twisted cord trim.

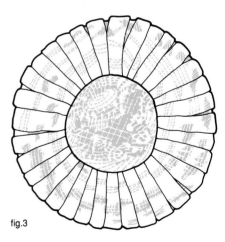

fig.3

a 2.5cm (1in) turning. Press the seam open and sew in the zipper. Cut away excess canvas, leaving 1.2cm (½in) of unsewn canvas for turning.
4 Tack the central fabric panel to each side of the needlepoint panels, close to the finished needlepoint. Tack the side fabric panels to the other side of the needlepoint panels. Machine into place, keeping as close to the finished needlepoint as possible. At this stage you can sew the cord, fringe or braid down the panel seams.
5 Tack the cushion backing to the front, right sides together. Machine in place. Turn through to the right side and sew on cord or braid by hand.

## GATHERED RUCHED BORDER CUSHION WITH CORD
Illustrated on page 107
**Materials**
1m (1¼yd) fabric 122cm (48in) wide

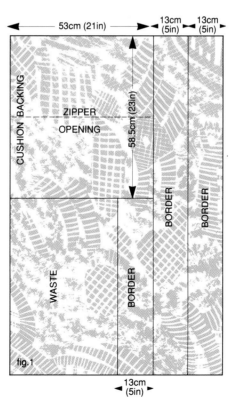

fig.1

## CUSHION WITH TWISTED CORD TRIM AND 'FROGS' IN EACH CORNER
Illustrated on page 42
**Materials**
0.5m (⅝yd) fabric 122cm (48in) wide or remnant slightly larger than cushion size
Zipper 8cm (3in) shorter than height of finished cushion

Twisted cord approx 142cm (56in) longer than the measurement around the cushion
Pins
Clear adhesive tape

**1–4** Follow steps 1–4 of Cushion with twisted cord trim.
**5** Sew on the cord by hand starting from the opening at the bottom and leaving a small 'tail', as in step 5 of Cushion with twisted cord trim. Sew to the corner and make a loop. Secure with a few stitches. Do this three times, making the centre loop a little larger than the others. Repeat this when you reach the other three corners. (Before cutting the cord, wrap the ends with adhesive tape to prevent them fraying.)
**6** Join the cord by weaving the ends together and securing with a few stitches. Wrap the join with adhesive tape before cutting away any excess cord. Tuck the ends into the opening and neaten by sewing in.

## CUSHION WITH RUCHED PIPING
Illustrated on page 103
**Materials**
0.5m (⅝yd) fabric 122cm (48in) wide
Zipper 8cm (3in) shorter than height of finished cushion
No. 5 piping cord to go around the cushion
Pins

**1** Stretch the needlepoint back to its original shape and cut away any excess canvas, leaving 1.2cm (½in) of unsewn canvas for turning.
**2** Cut out the cushion back to the same size as the canvas, adding 5cm (2in) to the width for the zipper seam. Fold the fabric in half from side to side and cut along the crease to form the zipper opening. At each end of the zipper opening stitch a 4cm (1½in) seam, taking a 2.5cm (1in) turning. Press the seam open and sew in the zipper.
**3** Cut enough 4.5cm (1¾in) strips to go around the cushion twice. Join the piping strips together. Insert the piping cord into the piping fabric, making sure to pin the cord to the fabric at the beginning. Machine together, pulling the piping cord through as you go (fig.1) to approximately double the fullness.
**4** Cut away the excess canvas, leaving 1.2cm (½in) of unsewn canvas for turning.

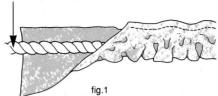

RUCHING CORD

fig.1

**5** Tack the ruched piping to the cushion close to the needlepoint. Sew the fabric ends together and join the piping cord ends together by wrapping cotton around each end. Then sew the ends together and machine into place.
**6** Tack the back to the cushion front, right sides together. Machine into place keeping close to the needlepoint. Over lock or double stitch the seams. Turn to the right side through the zipper opening.

## PLACEMAT
Illustrated on page 60
**Materials**
1.5m (1⅝yd) cord
Fabric for the backing 2.5cm (1in) bigger than the placemat
Pins

**1** Stretch the needlepoint back to its original shape.
**2** Cut away the excess canvas leaving 1.2cm (½in) for turning.
**3** Tack or pin the backing to the placemat right sides together, leaving a 25.5cm (10in) opening along one side. Machine into place. Trim the four corner turnings away (fig.1) so that the corners lay flat.

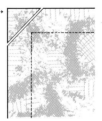

CUT CORNER →

fig.1

**4** Turn through to the right side and sew on the cord by hand, as in step 5 of Cushion with twisted cord trim, starting from the opening at the bottom and leaving a small 'tail'.

## BELT
Illustrated on page 47
**Materials**
Fabric for the backing, 2.5cm (1in) bigger all round than the belt
Buckle of your choice
Pins

**1** Stretch the needlepoint back to the original shape.
**2** Cut away the excess canvas, leaving 1.2cm (½in) turning.
**3** Cut the backing the same size as the needlepoint, including the unsewn canvas.
**4** Tack or pin the backing to the needlepoint right sides together, leaving a 30.5cm (12in) opening along one edge.
**5** Machine into place. Trim the four corner turnings away, as in step 5 of Placemat, so that the corners lay flat.
**6** Turn through to the right side, and press with damp cloth. Slip stitch the opening and sew on the buckle.

## SQUARE STOOL
Illustrated on page 69
**Materials**
Square stool (pad size 35.5 x 35.5cm (14 x 14in) – can be obtained from Glorafilia
0.7cm (¾in) tacks
Hammer
Staple gun (optional)

**1** Remove the stool top by undoing the screws recessed into the bottom of the frame.
**2** Lay the needlepoint right side down onto a flat surface. Lay the stool top pad down onto the needlepoint, making sure it is central. Temporarily tack the excess canvas as tightly as you can without distorting the needlepoint. Do this to all sides. Fold the excess canvas equally on each corner. Turn over to the right side and check that the needlepoint is fitting correctly. Now tack in place firmly or use a staple gun.

## RUG
Illustrated on page 83
**Materials**
Rug backing 2.5cm (1in) bigger than the size of the rug (can be obtained from Glorafilia)

**1** Lay the rug face downwards on a table, turn back the selvedges and stitch down.
**2** Lay the backing over the rug, smooth out and turn under surplus of about 1.25cm (½in) all round and stitch the edges of the backing to the edges of the rug. It is advisable to run a row of stitches across the width of the backing at about 2.5cm (1in) from each end of the backing to prevent it from bunching. Use the foam side for uncarpeted areas and the hessian side for carpeted areas.

# TRACE PATTERNS

CHILD ON A STOOL

*see page 132*

PARIS, A RAINY DAY

*see page 35*

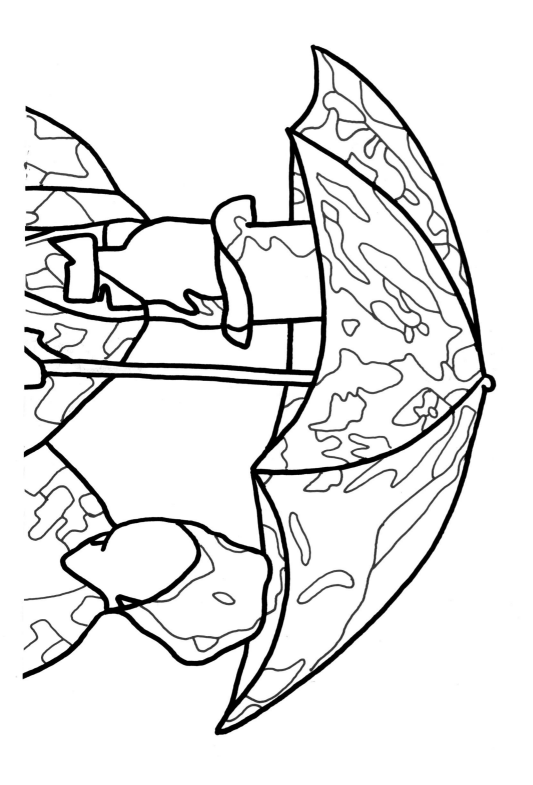

PEONIES

*see page 106*

WATERLILIES

*see page 102*

*Overleaf:*
IRISES

*see page 93*

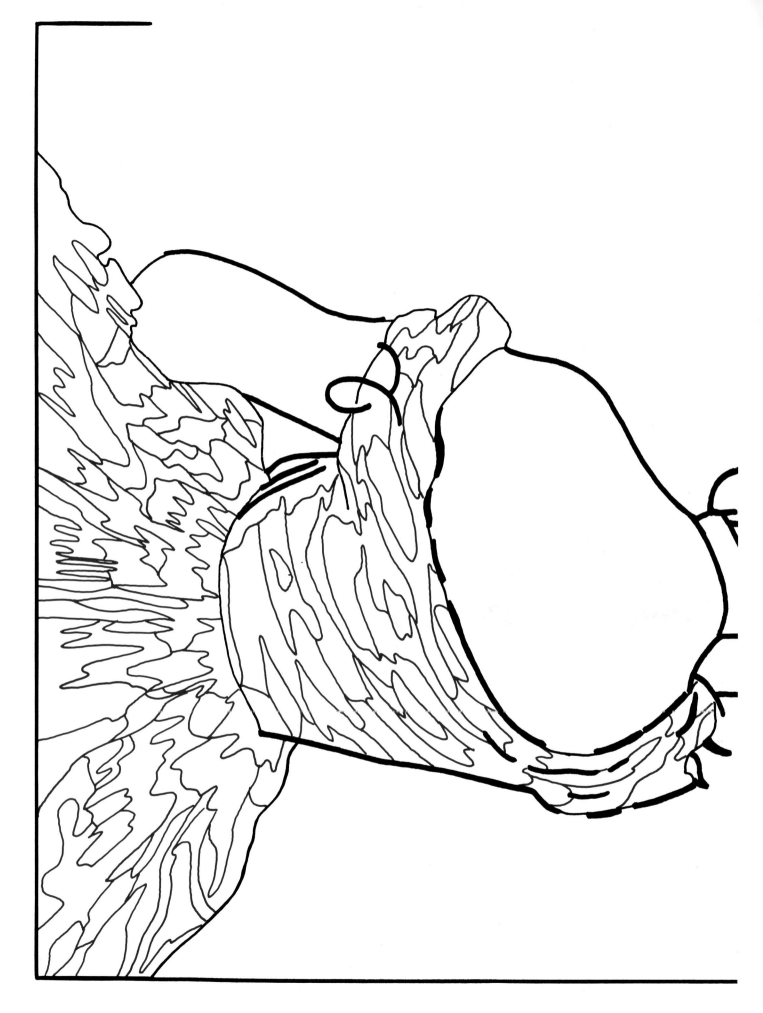

LADY AT HER TOILETTE
*see page 126*

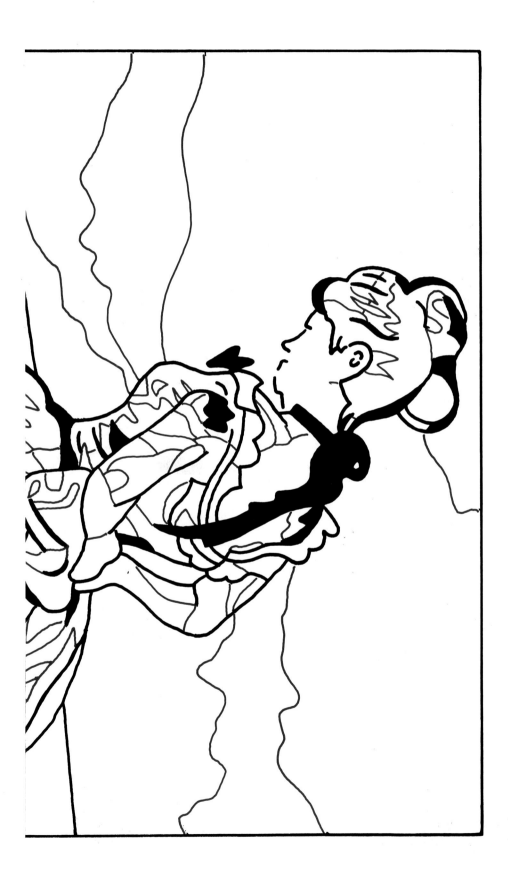

DANCER REHEARSING

*see page 122*

# INDEX

# ACKNOWLEDGMENTS

Our thanks to DMC for supplying us with the glorious yarns used and for all their help with this project.

Special thanks must go to all who sewed our samples so beautifully and with such care: Lynda Blundell, Mary Clark, Andrea Cooper, Dorothy de Lacy, Josephine Farhoumand, Evelyn Genis, Chris Gregory, Vicki Henley, Joyce Talbot and especially Daphne King, for her saintly patience! And with great thanks to our Glorafilia girls who were all, directly and indirectly, involved with the book.

Thanks to the following people for supplying materials for photography:
Ena Green Antiques, Alfie's Antique Market, 13–25 Church Street, London NW8 8DT.
Graham & Green, 4 and 7 Elgin Crescent, London W11.
Decorative Living, 55 New Kings Road, London SW6.
Gallery of Antique Costume and Textiles, 2 Church Street, London NW8.
Magpie, 152 Wandsworth Bridge Road, Fulham, London SW6.
Sandra Brunswick Antiques, Alfie's Antique Market, 13–25 Church Street, London NW8 8DT.
Harper & Toms, 13 Elgin Crescent, London W11.
Joanna and Hugh Holbeach
Polly Wiles
Joan Peters

We would also like to thank Jill and Paul Rudder for the loan of their house.

An enormous thank you goes to those at Claude Monet's house and garden at Giverny and in particular the head gardener, M. Gilbert Vahé, for help in making the photography an undeniable pleasure. Thank you also to the Château de Brécourt in Pacy-sur-Eure for inside location shots.

## MATERIALS AND KITS SERVICE

**Glorafilia** can provide all the materials needed to complete each project in this book: canvas cut to size and taped at the edges, the correct needles and enough yarn to complete the design, and various items of equipment that you may need.

### Yarn suppliers
For details of stockists and mail order sources of the yarns used in this book, please contact the following addresses:

### DMC Yarns
DMC Creative World Ltd, Pullman Road, Wigston, Leicestershire LE8 2DY. Tel: 0533 811040 Fax: 0533 813592.
DMC Needlecraft Pty. Ltd., P O Box 317, Earlswood NSW 2206, Australia. Tel: 255 93088 Fax: 255 95338.
The DMC Corporation, Port Kearny, Building 10, South Kearny, NJ 07032 USA. Tel: 201 589 0606 Fax: 201 589 8931.

### Complete kits
The following designs are also available as kits. They each contain canvas printed in full color, instructions, needles and all the necessary yarns.

Fans                       Irises
Waterlilies                Dancer
Lady at her Toilette       Peonies
Monet Poppies              Wisteria Rug
Monet's Garden             Woman in her Bath

A number of designs which are not featured as actual projects in the book are also available as kits:
Beach Scene (pages 22–23)
The Green Hat (pages 110–111)
Flag Irises (page 8)
Japanese Bridge (page 101)
If you would like further information, or to order kits or materials directly, write to:
Glorafilia Ltd, The Old Mill House, The Ridgeway, London NW7 4EB. Tel: 081 906 0212 Fax 081 959 6253.
Marsha Kear, 510 Weadley Road, King of Prussia, PA 19406, USA. Tel/Fax: 215 688 4864.

## PICTURE CREDITS

The publishers wish to thank the following for the use of photographs:
**The Bridgeman Art Library, London** for *The Artist's Garden at Giverny, Claude Monet Painting at the Edge of a Wood, Misty Morning, The Magpie, Lady with Fans, Lola de Valence, The Luncheon, Irises, Waterlily Pond, Pond with Waterlilies, Woman in her Bath, Sponging her Leg, Girl Reading.*
**Fogg Art Museum, Cambridge Massachusetts** for *Spring Bouquet*; **The Metroplitan Museum of Art, New York** for *The Cup of Tea*; **The Institute of Chicago, Stickney Fund** for *Lady at her Toilette*: **Flint Museum of Arts, Flint, Michigan** for *Lydia Working at a Tapestry Frame*; **Musée de l'Orangerie, Paris** for *Strawberries*; **Musée d'Orsay, Paris** for *Paris, A Rainy Day*; **Réunion des Musées Nationaux, Paris** for *Profile Portrait of Lydia Cassatt*; **Louvre, Paris** for *Peonies*; **Oskar Reinhart Collection** for *At the Café*; **Various private collections** for *The Seine at Marly, Bunch of Violets, Dancer Rehearsing* and *The Story*. Every effort has been made to contact them.